FROM THE RECIPE FILES OF THE
C.I.A.
THE CULINARY INSTITUTE OF AMERICA

BASED ON THE PUBLIC TELEVISION SERIES

MAJOR FUNDING PROVIDED BY CUISINART

ADDITIONAL FUNDING PROVIDED BY THERMOS

PRODUCED BY MARJORIE POORE PRODUCTIONS

MPP BOOKS

Distributed by Publishers Group West

Text and recipes copyright ©1996 by The Culinary Institute of America

Tim Ryan, Senior Vice President
Henry Woods, Project Manager

Photography by Dennis Gray
Photgraphs copyright © 1996 by Marjorie Poore Productions

Library of Congress Cataloging in Publication Data
Available

ISBN 0-9651095-0-X

Printed in Hong Kong

10 9 8 7 6 5 4 3 2 1

MPP Books
363 14th Avenue
San Francisco, CA 94118

Distributed by Publishers Group West

ACKNOWLEDGMENTS

The Culinary Institute of America is a private, not-for-profit educational institution committed to providing the world's best professional culinary arts and science education. This book and the accompanying second season of our public television series enable us to reach millions of people who may never have the opportunity to take classes at our Hyde Park or Napa Valley campuses. We would like to express our deepest appreciation to those who have made this effort possible:

Cuisinart and their team of professionals, for their vision in being the first company to step forward as a major sponsor and their continued commitment to the project.

Thermos, which demonstrated its commitment to the school by becoming an underwriter.

The Danny Kaye and Sylvia Fine Kaye Foundation, for providing the ideal theater in which to record the video series.

Our producer, Marjorie Poore, for her creativity, drive, talent, and belief in the CIA, and to her partner and business manager, Alec Fatalevich, for his role in making the project a reality.

Project manager Henry Woods, whose talents, organizational skills and tireless efforts kept everything running smoothly.

The faculty and staff of the CIA, who shared their knowledge so openly and freely, and who worked so long and hard on this special project.

Chef Elizabeth Briggs and the tremendous staff of student volunteers, too numerous to mention, for prepping food, organizing *mise en place*, and washing countless pots and pans.

The book's skillful contributors: Jessica Tyler Bard, for preparing the recipes for publication, Mary Deirdre Donovan, for editorial guidance, Joan Andrek, for her holiday research, and Maria Renz, for data entry.

The talented video production staff, who worked tirelessly both on and off location: Michel Bisson, Skip Thela, Alain Letourneau, Dana Degenhardt, and Steve Ackels.

And finally, all the present and future students of the CIA–including our new home viewers and readers–who are our reason for being.

Tim Ryan, Senior Vice President
The Culinary Institute of America

CONTENTS

Holidays and celebrations mean foods that require a personal touch. The chefs of The Culinary Institute of America have opened up their very own recipe files for you to explore in preparing these special meals for special times. In this volume, we are happy to include not only the secret recipe files of our Hyde Park, New York, campus, but for the very first time those from our new Greystone campus in St. Helena, California, as well. Whether from the East or West Coast, all the recipes illustrate our basic philosophy of serving local, fresh, and seasonal ingredients with care and enthusiasm. The Culinary Institute of America is pleased to reveal these outstanding recipes through the second season of its nationally broadcast public television series, _Cooking Secrets of the CIA_, to which this book is a companion.

Ah spring! No matter how you feel about the fall and winter seasons, it is almost impossible to ignore the optimism that comes with the season of renewal. Spring signals a fresh start for earth and all its creatures — with many holidays and celebrations to mark the occasion.

Perhaps the two most widely recognized spring holidays are Passover and Easter. Both have tremendous historical significance and are considered major holidays within the Jewish and Christian faiths. We will examine traditional foods and menus associated with each.

While most of us would not consider April 15 a joyous occasion, at the very least we breathe a sigh of relief when our taxes have been filed. In keeping with the spirit of the Internal Revenue Service, we have brought together several low-cost suggestions to please your appetites while nursing your slim wallets.

One of the many bounties of spring is the renewed abundance of fresh vegetables. Three vegetable jewels, asparagus, peas, and fiddlehead ferns, are used to enhance risotto and salmon, creating a royal spring menu.

Intertwined with our seasonal celebrations are reminders of our cultural diversity. As we approach the month of May, our neighbors to the south prepare for Cinco de Mayo, a Mexican fiesta that has found ready acceptance throughout America. We offer two Cinco menus to make the most of this holiday: Southwestern and Mexican.

May continues its celebration theme with Mother's Day and Memorial Day. The first was officially recognized not long after the turn of the century, and quickly became an annual rite of spring. Memorial Day, with its origins in the Civil War, carries some solemnity. However, it is also embraced as the "official" start to the summer cookout and grilling season, and the long, lazy days of fun to follow. We have plenty of delicious suggestions for enhancing both of these holidays.

We can't forget that spring and summer herald other celebrations as well — engagements, weddings, graduations, and the like — that are as much a part of the warmer weather as barbecues and beach parties. Helpful hints and great recipe ideas for our party buffet menu are sure to come in handy whether you're planning a significant affair or casual gathering.

The menu at the Wine Spectator's Greystone Restaurant is inspired by the healthful, flavorful, and fresh aspects of Mediterranean cuisine and is exemplified by our Father's Day menu. It is sure to please all generations of fathers in your family.

Heading into summer, we take a walk through the garden to absorb the wealth of menu opportunities that fresh fruits and vegetables present. Summer menus broadcast from Greystone include Seasonal Salads and Scrumptious Summer Desserts.

If there is one truly "American" celebration, both in origin and menu, it is Independence Day. Our All-American Fourth of July Meal provides a rendition of a classic New England clambake that you can make at home in any part of the country. We will also visit the culinary tradition that has merged with this holiday — the backyard barbecue — with our Summer Sizzle on the Grill menu. Shortly after our celebration of independence, the French recognize their own on Bastille Day. Our menu for a French Country Picnic offers great ideas that you can easily pack in a basket and bring along to your favorite spot in the park.

Some special summer delights are visited through recipes for a variety of summer sandwiches as well as sweet and savory summer fruits. We put the finishing touches on the season with late-summer vegetables and a labor-free, farewell-to-summer-party on Labor Day. Our final menu completes the celebratory cycle with traditional foods for Rosh Hashanah, the Jewish New Year.

Get ready for a year of wonderful culinary opportunities, with *From the Recipe Files of the CIA*.

PASSOVER

Chef Morey Kanner

"Tradition" is most evident at every Passover Seder — it is a joyous holiday that brings back fond memories from generation to generation. I used to watch my grandmother spend two hours cutting the fish by hand to prepare gefilte fish with beet horseradish. Nowadays, we have equipment that simplifies the way we prepare these dishes while allowing us to preserve the authentic flavors and textures. I prefer to keep one foot in tradition and the other in innovation. For example, I make gefilte fish using the traditional ingredients, but have re-interpreted the accompaniment by separating the beets from the horseradish, serving them as a preserve alongside the horseradish to enhance the appearance of the dish.

Chef Stacy Radin

Baking for Passover is always challenging, because desserts for this holiday may not be prepared with any grain or flour, or any leaveners such as yeast, baking powder, or baking soda. It is with this thought in mind that I chose to prepare a variety of macaroon cookies — a traditional cookie of the holiday that I remember being bought in cans and available only at this time of year!

HOMEMADE GEFILTE FISH WITH BEET PRESERVES AND FRESH HORSERADISH
Serves 8 as a first course

POACHING LIQUID
8 cups Fish Broth (page 107)
1 onion, thinly sliced
1 large carrot, sliced
1 bay leaf

GEFILTE FISH
1 pound pike fillets, diced and chilled
1 pound whitefish fillets, diced and chilled
1 large onion, grated
6 egg whites, chilled
2 teaspoons salt
½ teaspoon finely ground pepper
¼ cup ice water
½ cup matzo meal
Beet Preserves (recipe follows)
Fresh Horseradish (recipe follows)
5 green onions, white and green portions,
    cut into julienne
1 large carrot, cut into julienne

To make the poaching liquid: Combine all the poaching liquid ingredients in a large pot. Bring to a gentle simmer over medium-low heat. Simmer for 10 to 15 minutes.

To make the gefilte fish: Combine all the gefilte fish ingredients in a food processor and process for 15 seconds. Use a small serving spoon to scrape out a spoonful of the mixture against the side of the bowl. Using another small serving spoon, shape the gefilte fish into a dumpling by gently pushing the mixture off the other spoon and dropping it into the simmering poaching liquid. Continue until all of the fish mixture has been made into dumplings.

Cook the gefilte fish until all the dumplings float to the liquid's surface, about 10 to 12 minutes. Remove the pan from heat and let the dumplings cool in their poaching liquid for 30 minutes at room temperature. Refrigerate until the broth has jelled, about 4 hours or overnight.

Using a slotted spoon, carefully remove the dumplings from the jelled broth and place on chilled plates. Serve with beet preserves, fresh horseradish, julienned green onion, and carrot.

BEET PRESERVES
Serves 8; makes about 1½ cups

1 cup grated peeled raw beets
¼ cup cider vinegar
¼ cup sugar
½ small onion, grated
1 teaspoon salt
¼ teaspoon ground pepper

Combine all of the ingredients in a small nonreactive pan and simmer gently over medium heat for about 15 to 20 minutes, or until all the liquid has been absorbed. Chill well before serving.

Chef's Tip: Beet preserves may be made up to 3 days in advance. To hold them, put them in a clean container, cover and refrigerate.

FRESH HORSERADISH
Serves 8; makes about ½ cup

Prepare this horseradish at least 1 day in advance so its flavor has time to develop.

One 6-inch-piece horseradish root,
**   peeled and cut into ¾-inch pieces**
½ cup water
1 teaspoon salt
1 tablespoon cider vinegar

Grate the horseradish with the water in a blender until very finely shredded. Scrape down the blender's sides with a rubber spatula. (See Chef's Tips to prepare in a food processor.) Strain off any excess liquid and transfer the horseradish to a bowl. Add the salt and vinegar and stir to combine. Place in a clean jar, cover, and refrigerate overnight. Serve cold.

Chef's Tips: To make horseradish in a food processor, fit the processor with the fine grating disc. Peel and cut the horseradish so that it will fit through the feed tube. Grate the horseradish in the processor and transfer it to a bowl.
Add the salt and vinegar. The water may be omitted.
Store in a covered container in the refrigerator for up to 3 days.

MATZO BALLS IN CHICKEN BROTH
KNAIDLACH
Serves 8 as a soup course

MATZO BALLS
   1¾ cups matzo meal
   6 eggs, beaten
   1 cup water
   2 teaspoons salt
   2 teaspoons finely ground pepper
   ½ cup rendered chicken fat, melted (page107)

   8 cups Chicken Broth (page 107)
   Salt and freshly ground pepper to taste
   Optional garnish: see Chef's Tips

To make the matzo balls: Combine the matzo meal, eggs, water, salt, and pepper in a food processor. Process for 15 to 20 seconds. Add the chicken fat and pulse just until the fat is incorporated. Transfer to a bowl, cover, and refrigerate for 20 to 30 minutes.

Bring a pot of lightly salted water to a simmer over low heat. Wet your hands and form the matzo mixture into balls about 2 inches in diameter. (For *Knaidlach mit Neshomes,* see Chef's Tips.) Gently drop the balls into the simmering water. Cover the pot and simmer for 20 minutes, or until firm and cooked through.

Meanwhile, bring the chicken broth to a simmer in a large saucepan. Season with salt and pepper. When the matzo balls are cooked, transfer them with a slotted spoon to warmed soup plates or bowls. Ladle the hot broth onto the matzo balls, garnish if you like, and serve.

Chef's Tips: A garnish of thinly sliced green onion (green and white portions), cooked peas, and/or julienne-cut blanched carrot and parsnip adds greatly to this dish.

To make Knaidlach mit Neshomes *(Matzo Balls with a Surprise), form the matzo balls around a bit of browned onion or chicken cracklings.*

PAN-ROASTED BREAST OF DUCK WITH GOLDEN RAISIN AND ORANGE SAUCE
Serves 8 as a main course

The duck broth should be made 1 or 2 days in advance.

4 ducks, about 4 to 5 pounds each

GOLDEN RAISIN AND ORANGE SAUCE
   8 cups Duck Broth (page 108)
   1 tablespoon cornstarch
   2 tablespoons cold water
   2 tablespoons golden raisins
   ¼ cup brandy or Cognac
   ¼ cup sugar
   Juice of 4 oranges
   ¼ cup cider vinegar
   1 tablespoon currant jelly
   Salt and freshly ground pepper to taste

   Julienned zest of 4 oranges, blanched (page 105), for garnish

Cut the breasts away from the duck and trim away any excess fat. Wrap the breasts well in plastic wrap and refrigerate them until ready to cook. Reserve the legs and carcasses to make the broth.

To make the sauce: Place the broth in a large saucepan and simmer over medium heat until reduced to 2 cups. Combine the cornstarch and cold water in a small bowl and mix well. Add this mixture to the reduced broth, whisking constantly. Simmer 1 to 2 minutes, or until the broth is thickened. Set aside and keep warm.

Combine the raisins with the brandy or Cognac to plump while making the rest of the sauce. Combine the sugar and 1 teaspoon of the orange juice in a medium, heavy nonreactive sauté pan and cook over medium heat without stirring. Once the sugar has begun to melt, stir occasionally until the sugar is completely melted and is golden brown, about 8 minutes.

Immediately add the vinegar and continue to cook until reduced by half.

Add the remaining orange juice to the reduced sugar. Drain the brandy or Cognac from the raisins and add it to the orange juice mixture. Simmer until reduced by half. Add the thickened broth, drained raisins, and jelly. Add the salt and pepper. Set the sauce aside and keep warm while preparing the duck breasts.

To cook the duck breasts: Preheat the oven to 350°F. Season the breasts with salt and pepper. Heat two 10-inch ovenproof sauté pans over high heat. Add the breasts in a single layer, skin-side down. Reduce the heat to medium-low and cook until the skin is nicely browned and crisp, about 4 to 5 minutes.

Transfer the pans to the oven and roast for about 10 minutes, or until an instant-read thermometer inserted in the duck registers 165°F. Transfer the breasts to a wire rack, skin-side up, and let them rest for 5 minutes before slicing.

Meanwhile, pour off the fat from the pans. Place the pans on the stove over medium heat and add the golden raisin and orange sauce to both pans. Stir to release any reduced drippings from the bottom of the pans. Pour the sauce into one pan and bring it to a simmer. Taste and adjust the seasoning with salt and pepper, if necessary.

To serve, slice each breast thinly on the bias. Fan out the slices on warmed serving plates and spoon the golden raisin and orange sauce over each breast. Garnish with orange zest and serve warm.

CHOCOLATE MACAROONS
Makes about 30 macaroons

1 cup almond flour (see Chef's Tips)
1 cup powdered sugar
½ cup unsweetened cocoa powder
4 egg whites
2 tablespoons granulated sugar

Sift the almond flour, powdered sugar, and cocoa powder together into a large bowl.

Using an electric mixer on high speed, beat the egg whites and sugar until stiff peaks form. Using a rubber spatula, gently fold the sifted dry ingredients into the egg white mixture.

Line baking sheets with parchment paper. Fill a pastry bag fitted with a No. 6 tip (½-inch-diameter opening) with the chocolate mixture. Pipe into rounds 1½ inches in diameter and about 1 inch apart.

Preheat the oven to 400°F. While the oven heats, let the macaroons dry for 20 minutes at room temperature to develop a crust.

Bake until the macaroons are puffed and have cracks on the upper surface, about 7 minutes. Transfer the macaroons, still on the parchment paper, to a wire rack to cool completely. When cool, they will lift off easily.

Chef's Tips: Store macaroons in an airtight container at room temperature for up to 2 days.

Almond flour may be purchased in specialty foods shops or natural foods stores.

EASTER DINNER
ITALIAN STYLE

Chef Joe DiPerri

Easter Sunday is a day of great celebration. It signals the end of fasting, and a spiritual renewal for the faithful. I have created a Italian Easter dinner menu for your own feast. The lamb and asparagus are not only traditional but are at their prime in the early spring. Ravioli are featured here as part of the feast, since this richly filled and elaborately prepared pasta was certainly not part of the minimal Lenten menu. All Italians eat bread with their meals and the bread salad Tuscan style *(panzanella)* is a creative way to use the leftovers. It's so good, it's worth planning ahead to be sure you have some day-old bread.

Buon Appetito!

LAMB CHOPS WITH PARMESAN AND MUSHROOM RAGOUT
COSTOLETTO DI AGNELLO CON PARMIGIANO E RAGÙ DI FUNGHI
Serves 8 as a main course

LAMB SAUCE

6 pounds meaty lamb bones and trimmings
1 large onion, coarsely chopped
1 carrot, coarsely chopped
1 stalk celery, coarsely chopped
1 teaspoon tomato paste
½ cup plus 6 tablespoons dry red wine
8 cups Brown Veal Stock (page 106)
1 each small parsley, rosemary, marjoram,
    and thyme sprig
5 to 6 garlic cloves, roasted and peeled (page 103)
2 tablespoons cornstarch

16 lamb rib chops, frenched (see Chef's Tip)
Salt and freshly ground pepper to taste
4 teaspoons olive oil
1 small rosemary sprig
2½ tablespoons balsamic vinegar
Shaved Parmesan as needed (page 104),
    or ½ cup grated Parmesan
Mushroom Ragout (recipe follows)

To make the sauce: Preheat the oven to 350°F. Put the bones, trimmings and vegetables in a roasting pan and roast for 15 to 20 minutes, turning occasionally, or until they are golden brown.

Spoon off the excess fat. Place the pan over medium heat. Stir in the tomato paste and cook for 2 minutes. Add the ½ cup red wine and stir to release all of the drippings from the bottom of the pan. Add the stock, herbs, and garlic, and simmer for about 10 to 15 minutes, or until the liquid is reduced by half (about 4 cups).

Combine the 6 tablespoons red wine with the cornstarch in a small bowl and stir well. Bring the reduced stock to a boil. Whisk in the cornstarch mixture, stirring constantly, and simmer until thickened into a sauce. Strain the sauce through a sieve into a saucepan and keep warm. (See Chef's Tips.)

To prepare the lamb chops: Preheat the oven to 450°F. Season the chops with salt and pepper. Heat the oil in a large sauté pan over high heat until the surface shimmers. Sear the chops, working in batches, for about 3 to 4 minutes on the first side, or until a deep brown, then turn and brown on the second side. As the chops are searing, add a few leaves from the rosemary sprig to the pan to "perfume" the chops.

Arrange the chops in a single layer in a baking pan. Add enough of the lamb sauce to cover the bottom of the pan. (Reserve the remaining sauce to serve on the side.) Stir in the vinegar. Top each chop with Parmesan to cover. Bake for about 2 minutes, or until the cheese melts.

Serve the chops with the mushroom ragout and drizzle with lamb sauce from the baking pan. Pass the reserved sauce on the side in a heated gravy boat or small pitcher.

Chef's Tips: "Frenching" is the term used for the process of scraping the ends of the rib bones completely clean. This makes them neater, so they can be picked up with the fingers. Your butcher can do this for you. Eliminating this step will not affect the flavor or cooking time of the dish, however.

The sauce can be prepared up to 4 days in advance. To store it, stop just before adding the cornstarch. Strain the sauce into a clean container. Cool to room temperature, cover, and refrigerate (or freeze it for up to 2 months). Return the sauce to a boil before adding the cornstarch.

MUSHROOM RAGOUT
RAGÙ DI FUNGHI
Serves 8; makes about 4 cups

¼ cup olive oil
2 pounds mixed wild mushrooms
    (cremini, shiitake, and/or oyster),
    stemmed and quartered
1 pint pearl onions, parboiled and peeled (page 103)
4 baking potatoes, peeled, scooped into balls
    with a melon baller, and parboiled (page 103)
¼ cup Chicken Broth (page 107)
4 tablespoons (½ stick) unsalted butter
Salt and freshly ground pepper to taste

Heat the olive oil in a large sauté pan over medium heat. Add the mushrooms, pearl onions, and potatoes and sauté for 2 to 3 minutes. Add the broth and butter and continue cooking until liquid has thickened and the potatoes are tender, about 5 minutes. Season with salt and pepper.

BREAD SALAD TUSCAN STYLE
PANZANELLA ALLA TOSCANA
Serves 8 as a salad course

DRESSING
> 6 tablespoons extra-virgin olive oil
> 2 tablespoons red wine vinegar
> 2 garlic cloves, minced
> Salt and freshly ground pepper to taste
> Shaved Parmesan (page 104) as needed,
>   or ½ cup grated Parmesan for garnish
> Extra-virgin olive oil for drizzling
>
> ½ pound day-old crusty Italian bread or focaccia,
>   cut into ½-inch dice (about 4 cups)
> 5 plum tomatoes, seeded and cut into ½-inch dice
>   (see Chef's Tips)
> 2 seedless cucumbers, peeled and cut into
>   ½-inch dice (see Chef's Tips)
> 2 red onions, thinly sliced
> Leaves from 1 bunch basil, cut into shreds

To make the dressing: Whisk all the dressing ingredients together in a small bowl.

Mix together the bread, tomatoes, cucumber, onions, and basil in a large bowl. Pour the dressing over the bread mixture and toss the salad to coat all the ingredients evenly. Serve on a chilled platter or individual plates. Garnish with Parmesan and drizzle with extra-virgin olive oil.

Chef's Tips: This rustic salad is traditionally prepared with the skin left on the tomatoes. To remove the seeds, cut each tomato in half crosswise, hold the tomato half upside down over a bowl, and gently squeeze out the seeds.

Seedless cucumbers are often sold as European, burpless, or hothouse cucumbers. If seedless varieties are unavailable, use regular cucumbers; cut them in half and scoop out the seeds before cutting into dice.

CHEESE RAVIOLI WITH ASPARAGUS
RAVIOLI DI FORMAGGIO CON ASPARAGI
Serves 8 to 10 as a first course, 6 to 8 as a main course

CHEESE FILLING
> 1 pound ricotta cheese
> 1 egg
> ¼ cup grated Parmesan
> ¼ cup grated pecorino romano
> ¼ cup chopped fresh parsley
> Salt and freshly ground pepper to taste
>
> 1 egg
> 1 tablespoon water
> 1½ pounds Fresh Pasta Sheets (recipe follows)
> 1¼ cup (½ stick) unsalted butter at room
>   temperature, cut into pieces

GARNISH
> 40 asparagus tips, blanched (page 103), stalks reserved
> 3 tablespoons unsalted butter
> Asparagus Sauce (recipe follows)
> Grated Parmesan to taste

To make the filling: Combine all the filling ingredients in a medium bowl. Cover and refrigerate while making the ravioli.

To make the ravioli by hand: Whisk together the egg and water to make an egg wash. Lay out a sheet of pasta on a work surface. Place ½ tablespoon of filling every 2 inches on the pasta sheet. Brush the egg wash around the mounds of filling and lay a second sheet of pasta on top. Press down with your fingers in between the mounds to seal them off. Use a sharp knife or fluted pie crust cutter to cut out the ravioli. Repeat with the remaining filling and pasta sheets. Or, use a ravioli press or the attachment for your pasta machine.

Cook the ravioli in a large pot of salted boiling water for 5 to 8 minutes, or until al dente. Drain the ravioli well and immediately transfer them to a bowl with the ¼ cup of butter. Toss or stir gently until the ravioli are coated with butter.

To serve, combine the asparagus tips and butter in a small sauté pan and warm over medium heat. Serve the ravioli on warmed plates with the warm sauce. Garnish with the warm asparagus tips, sprinkle with Parmesan, and serve at once.

Chef's Tip: The ravioli may be frozen for up to 4 weeks before cooking. Do not defrost; cook the frozen ravioli for 8 to 10 minutes, or until al dente.

ASPARAGUS SAUCE
Serves 8; makes about 3 cups

40 asparagus stalks (reserved from garnish,
    preceding recipe)
1 cup Chicken Broth (page 107)
1 cup (2 sticks) unsalted butter,
    cut into pieces
Salt and freshly ground pepper to taste

Cut off the woody end of each stalk and peel any tough skin from the stalks. Cut the stalks into ½-inch lengths. Combine the chicken broth, asparagus stalks, and butter in a medium saucepan. Simmer over medium heat until tender, 5 to 8 minutes. Purée the mixture until smooth using a hand-held blender, a food processor, or a blender. Season with salt and pepper. Strain through a sieve, if desired, and keep warm.

FRESH PASTA SHEETS
Makes 1½ pounds pasta

4 cups all-purpose flour
5 eggs
1 teaspoon salt

To mix the dough in a food processor: Place all the ingredients in a food processor. Pulse until mixture is very coarse and grainy; it should not form a ball. The mixture should pack easily when pressed together. If it is too dry, add water, 1 teaspoon at a time, until the correct consistency is reached. If it is too wet, add additional flour. (For hand-mixing instructions, see Chef's Tips.)

To roll the pasta: Cut the dough into 8 equal pieces. Work with one piece at a time and keep the remainder covered with plastic wrap. Roll the dough out with a rolling pin to flatten slightly. Open the pasta machine to its widest setting and feed the dough through the machine. Reroll the dough, narrowing the setting each time, until the sheet is very thin, about ¹⁄₁₆-inch thick. Repeat with the remaining dough.

Place the finished sheets on a flour-dusted baking sheet and cover loosely with a kitchen towel.

Chef's Tips: Pasta dough is very firm. While it is possible to mix and roll it by hand, a food processor and a pasta machine make the job much easier.

To mix the dough by hand: Place the flour and salt in a large bowl. Make a well in the center and add the eggs. Using a fork, blend the flour into the eggs until a stiff but manageable dough forms. If necessary, add water, 1 teaspoon at a time. Once the dough is mixed, remove it to a lightly floured work surface and knead until a smooth, homogenous dough is formed. Let the dough rest for 10 minutes before rolling.

Pasta dough, rolled or unrolled, can be stored up to 1 week if it has been wrapped tightly in plastic wrap and refrigerated.

EASTER SWEETS

Certified Master Pastry Chef Joe McKenna

The association between Easter eggs and the Easter rabbit is directly attributable to German folklore. The rabbit is considered the most prolific of animals, and it made sense that eggs, a sign of fertility, would be carried to and fro by rabbits. This tradition continues today, as evidenced by the popularity of chocolate bunnies and candy eggs. Chocolate bunnies and eggs are a bit difficult to make at home, so I offer other chocolate treats such as chocolate-covered almonds or candied orange peels.

My recipe for poached meringue "eggs" with fresh-fruit salsa offers an updated, lighter version of the classic French *"oeufs à la niege,"* or snow eggs. It makes a very tasty and colorful finish to any meal.

CANDIED ORANGE PEELS
Makes about 6 dozen pieces of candied peels

The candied orange peels should be prepared 3 to 4 days before they are dipped in chocolate.

6 naval oranges

SYRUP
4 cups sugar
3 cups water
¾ cup light corn syrup

CHOCOLATE COATING
1 pound semisweet chocolate, chopped
1 pound milk chocolate, chopped

Cut the oranges into quarters. Remove the pulp, leaving as much pith (the white portion under the skin) on the peel as possible. Place the peels in a medium saucepan and cover with cold water. Bring to a boil, then drain off the water. Repeat this process 3 more times, or until the peels can be easily pierced with a knife. Drain thoroughly and set aside.

To make the syrup: While blanching the orange peels, combine all the syrup ingredients in a large, heavy saucepan and bring to a boil over high heat. Set aside.

Add the blanched peels to the sugar syrup and bring to a simmer over medium heat. Reduce heat to low and simmer for 1 hour, or until the orange peels appear somewhat shiny and slightly translucent. Transfer the peels and syrup to a medium bowl and let cool to room temperature. Cover and refrigerate for at least 3 to 4 days before coating with chocolate.

To temper the chocolate: Melt two thirds of the semisweet chocolate in a double boiler over barely simmering water. It should reach 115°F. Remove double boiler from heat. Add the remaining chocolate and stir until the chocolate cools to 90°F. It is now "tempered." (For more information on tempering, see page 105.)

Remove the orange peels from the syrup with a slotted spoon. Pat dry with a cloth towel and cut the orange peels into ⅜-by-2-inch strips.

Dip one half of each orange strip into the tempered semisweet chocolate, wiping off the excess on the bowl's rim. Place the strips on baking sheets lined with parchment paper or aluminum foil.

Temper the milk chocolate as you did the semisweet chocolate, stirring constantly. When the semisweet chocolate has set on the orange peels, after about 3 minutes, dip the uncoated half in the milk chocolate. Allow the chocolates to dry thoroughly on the baking sheets before serving.

Chef's Tip: Store the peels in an airtight container in a cool, dry place for up to 2 weeks. Do not refrigerate.

CHOCOLATE-COVERED ALMONDS
Makes about 2 pounds chocolate-covered almonds

3 tablespoons water
¾ cup sugar
1 pound (about 3 cups) whole blanched almonds
1 tablespoon unsalted butter
12 ounces semisweet chocolate, chopped
½ cup unsweetened cocoa powder

Combine the water and the sugar in a small saucepan. Cook over high heat, stirring, until the sugar dissolves and the syrup registers 228°F to 230°F on a candy thermometer, or until a small amount of sugar syrup on the end of a wooden spoon forms a long "thread" when it is pinched between your thumb and forefinger and your fingers are drawn apart.

Remove the saucepan from heat and add the almonds to the syrup. Stir the nuts until they are individually coated and look crystallized (they should have a somewhat milky color and grainy texture). Return the saucepan to medium heat and cook, stirring constantly with a wooden spoon, until the sugar coating becomes a medium to dark golden brown and makes a crackling sound, about 5 minutes. Add the butter to the nuts. Stir well to coat evenly. Pour the almonds onto a baking sheet and carefully separate them. Let the nuts cool in the freezer for about 3 minutes.

Melt the chocolate in a double boiler over barely simmering water, stirring constantly with a wooden spoon until smooth.

Put the nuts in a large bowl. Pour one third of the melted chocolate over the nuts, stirring constantly until the chocolate firms up; the nuts will become a lumpy mass. Continue stirring until they separate again. Pour the nuts back onto baking sheet and put in the refrigerator for 5 minutes. Repeat this process twice more, until all of the chocolate has been incorporated. Reserve the bowl.

Warm the bowl used to coat the nuts over barely simmering water just until the chocolate clinging to its sides melts. Return the nuts to the bowl and stir until the chocolate coating on the nuts starts to melt. Pour the cocoa into a second bowl and transfer the nuts to the cocoa. Stir with a wooden spoon until the almonds are lightly coated. Place the nuts in a sieve and shake off the excess cocoa powder. Spread the nuts out on a baking sheet and let the chocolate and cocoa firm up before serving.

Chef's Tip: Store the nuts in an airtight container in a cool, dry place for up to 2 weeks. Do not refrigerate.

DRIED FRUIT AND NUT CLUSTERS
Makes about 10 dozen clusters

1 pound white chocolate, chopped
½ cup dried currants
½ cup slivered dried apricots
½ cup halved unsalted pistachios
½ cup slivered almonds, toasted (page 104)

Line a baking sheet with parchment paper or aluminum foil. Melt two thirds of the chocolate in a double boiler over barely simmering water, stirring constantly, until the chocolate reaches 115°F. on an instant-read thermometer. Remove the double boiler from heat. Add the remaining chocolate and stir until it cools to 90°F. Keep the container over warm water to maintain the 90°F temperature while you shape the clusters.

Place about ½ cup chocolate in a pastry bag fitted with a ¼-inch tip. Pipe the chocolate onto the baking sheet in quarter-sized circles. (If you don't have a pastry bag, use a spoon to spread the chocolate.) While the chocolate is warm and fluid, arrange the dried fruits and nuts evenly over the surface of the chocolate "coins."

Continue until all of the chocolate has been used. Let the chocolate set completely before serving.

Chef's Tips: Any combination of dried fruits and nuts may be used. Also, any type of chocolate may be used: milk, white, semisweet, or bittersweet.

The clusters may be stored, covered, in a cool, dry place for up to 2 weeks. Do not refrigerate.

POACHED MERINGUE "EGGS" WITH FRESH FRUIT SALSA
Serves 8

8 egg whites
1¼ cups sugar
2 cups milk
Seeds from ½ vanilla bean (page 102)
Fresh Fruit Salsa (recipe follows)
8 mint sprigs for garnish

Cut out four 10-inch circles of parchment paper or waxed paper.

To make the meringue: Using an electric mixer or a whisk, beat the egg whites with 2 tablespoons of the sugar in a large bowl until soft peaks form. While still whipping, gradually add 1 cup of the sugar and the vanilla seeds and whip until stiff, but not dry, peaks form.

Combine the milk and the remaining 2 tablespoons sugar in a 10-inch sauté pan. (See Chef's Tip.) Warm over low heat until the mixture registers 140°F on an instant-read thermometer. (There should be no bubbles visible on the surface, and a small amount of steam should be rising from the surface.)

Using 2 large tablespoons or an oval ice cream scoop, shape the meringue into 6 "egg" shapes and place them on a parchment or waxed paper circle. Flip the circle over onto the hot milk and peel back the paper to release the "eggs." Poach the "eggs" for about 2 minutes on each side. Using a slotted spoon, carefully remove them and place on paper towels to drain slightly. Repeat with the remaining meringue to make 24 "eggs."

Divide the fruit salsa among dessert plates or soup plates and place 3 "eggs" on each bed of salsa. Garnish with a mint sprig.

Chef's Tip: The scraped vanilla bean pod may be added to the poaching liquid for additional flavor.

FRESH FRUIT SALSA
Serves 8; makes about 5 cups

3 slices honeydew melon, peeled and cut into
    small dice (about 1½ cups)
1 papaya, peeled and cut into small dice (about 1 cup)
1 mango, peeled, cut away from the pit,
    and cut into small dice (about 1 cup)
1 pint strawberries, hulled and cut into ¼-inch dice
    (about 1½ cups)
¼ cup passion fruit juice (page 105)
2 tablespoons minced fresh mint

SYRUP
¾ cup Amaretto
1½ cups fresh orange juice
¾ cup sugar

Combine the diced fruit with the passion fruit juice and mint in a large bowl and toss together. Let sit at room temperature while making the syrup.

To make the syrup: Combine all the syrup ingredients in a small saucepan. Cook over medium heat until the mixture has reduced to the consistency of maple syrup, about 8 minutes. Let cool slightly. Add the fruit mixture to the syrup and stir to combine. Cover and refrigerate until needed.

Chef's Tip: Other fresh seasonal fruits may be used in this recipe. Try peaches, apricots, plums, or kiwi.

COOKING AFTER TAXES

Chef Eve Felder

When T. S. Eliot wrote "April is the cruelest month," could he have been referring to our annual national "ante up to Uncle Sam?" I like to celebrate the end of another tax year with a dinner party, even though I know I have to tighten my belt and keep an eye on the budget while grocery shopping. My "cooking after taxes" menu invites frugality without sacrificing taste, appeal, and seasonality. Spring greens with cannellini beans, lemony chicken thighs with polenta, and a dessert of rhubarb make up a menu of dishes that are homey, delicious, and comforting, yet still have a touch of elegance.

SPRING GREENS AND CANNELLINI GRATIN
Serves 8 as a side dish or light entree

2 cups dried cannellini, white kidney,
    or Great Northern beans, soaked (page 102)
½ small onion, in a single piece
½ small carrot, in a single piece
1 thyme sprig
1 bay leaf
1½ teaspoons salt
Freshly ground pepper to taste
1 tomato, peeled, chopped, and seeded
    (about 1 cup), page 103
2 pounds chard or collard greens,
    rinsed and drained (see Chef's Tip)
1 tablespoon olive oil
1 teaspoon red pepper flakes
2 garlic cloves, minced
2 cups lightly toasted bread crumbs (page 104)

Combine the beans, onion, carrot, thyme, and bay leaf in a large pot. Add fresh cold water to cover the beans by 2 inches. Bring to a boil, then reduce heat to a simmer and cook for 15 to 20 minutes. Add the 1½ teaspoons salt and cook 20 to 30 minutes longer, or until the beans are completely tender (creamy and soft inside) but not falling apart. Drain the beans, reserving the cooking liquid. Remove and discard the onion, carrot, bay leaf, and thyme. Combine the beans in a bowl with 1 cup of the reserved cooking liquid and the chopped tomatoes.

Taste and adjust the seasoning with salt and pepper.

Preheat the oven to 350°F. Chop the greens into ½-inch pieces, keeping the stems and leaves separate. Heat 1 tablespoon of the olive oil in a large sauté pan over medium heat. Add the stems to the pan first and cook until they are wilted. Add the leaves and salt to taste, and continue to sauté, tossing occasionally, until the greens are wilted and tender, about 10 to 12 minutes. Add the pepper flakes and garlic and cook for 1 minute, or until the aroma of the garlic is released.

Combine the greens with the beans and tomatoes and mix thoroughly. Put the mixture in a 9-by-13-inch baking dish or a 1½-quart ceramic casserole and top with the bread crumbs. Bake for about 45 minutes, or until the crumbs are golden brown and the entire dish is very hot. If the crumbs begin to brown before the cooking time is complete, cover the pan loosely with aluminum foil. Serve hot.

Chef's Tip: Feel free to experiment with other cooking greens, such as escarole, tat soi (flat black cabbage), or turnip, dandelion, or beet greens. Cooking times may vary.

BRAISED CHICKEN WITH LEMON ZEST, OLIVES, AND CREAMY POLENTA
Serves 8 as a main course

GREMOLATA
½ bunch flat-leaf parsley,
    stemmed and coarsely chopped
Zest of 1 lemon, minced
1 garlic clove, minced

16 chicken thighs
Kosher salt and freshly ground pepper to taste
¼ cup olive oil
2 onions, cut into medium dice
4 garlic cloves, thinly sliced
32 green olives, preferably picholine
Six large pieces lemon zest (see Chef's Tip)
4 thyme sprigs
2 bay leaves
3½ cups Chicken Broth, or as needed (page 107),
    heated
Creamy Polenta (recipe follows)

To make the gremolata: Stir all the gremolata ingredients together in a small bowl. Cover and refrigerate while preparing the chicken.

Preheat the oven to 400°F. Season the chicken with salt and pepper. Heat the olive oil in a large, heavy skillet over medium heat. Add the thighs, skin-side down (work in batches to avoid crowding the pan). Sauté for about 3 to 5 minutes, or until well browned. Remove the thighs and set aside. Repeat with the remaining thighs.

Pour off half of the olive oil. Add the onions to the pan and sauté until translucent, about 5 to 7 minutes. Add the garlic and sauté for 1 minute, or until the aroma is released. Add the olives, lemon zest, thyme, and bay leaves, and stir until combined.

Spread the onion mixture in an even layer in a large baking dish. Place the thighs on top of the mixture in a single layer, skin-side down. Add enough hot chicken broth to come halfway up the thighs. Cover the pan tightly with a lid or aluminum foil and bake for 20 minutes. Remove the cover and turn the thighs skin-side up. Continue cooking, uncovered, until the skin is slightly crisp and the meat is fork-tender with no trace of pink remaining, about 20 minutes.

Transfer the chicken to a platter and keep warm in a 200°F oven while finishing the sauce. Strain the braising liquid through a sieve into a small pan and spoon off all the visible fat. Remove and discard the zest, bay leaves, and thyme sprigs from the onion mixture and scatter it over the chicken. Spoon off all the visible fat from the reserved liquid and simmer over medium-high heat until reduced by about half.

Serve the chicken and onions onto warmed plates. Spoon the sauce generously over each portion and top with the gremolata. Serve with the polenta.

Chef's Tip: Use a vegetable peeler to shave off large pieces of lemon zest that measure about ½-inch square. Be sure to cut away only the colored portion of the skin, as the white pith is quite bitter.

CREAMY POLENTA
Serves 8 to 10; makes about 10 cups

4 cups **Chicken Broth** (page 107)
4 cups **water**
1½ teaspoons **salt**
2 cups **polenta** (coarsely ground yellow cornmeal)
2 tablespoons **unsalted butter**

Combine the broth, water, and salt in a large saucepan. Bring to a rapid boil over high heat and slowly add the polenta, stirring constantly. Cook, stirring constantly, until the polenta begins to thicken.

Reduce heat to medium and continue stirring until the polenta begins to bubble. Reduce heat to low to a gentle simmer. Continue cooking for 45 minutes, stirring occasionally. Add the butter and stir until melted. The finished polenta should be loose enough to easily pour from a spoon. If it is too thick, adjust the consistency by adding hot water or broth. Serve hot.

Chef's Tip: Polenta may be poured onto a greased baking sheet, spread into an even layer, and refrigerated overnight. The firm polenta can then be cut into a variety of desired shapes using a knife or cookie cutters. It can be sautéed or grilled, then dusted with grated cheese or topped with a sauce, if you wish.

RHUBARB CRISP
Serves 8

This dish reminds me of the years I worked at Chez Panisse. It was adapted from my friend and colleague Lindsey Remolif Shere's book, *Chez Panisse Desserts* (Random House).

2 pounds **rhubarb**, cut into ½-inch lengths
    (about 6 cups)
1 cup **granulated sugar**
3½ tablespoons **flour**

TOPPING
1 cup **all-purpose flour**
⅓ cup **lightly packed brown sugar**
1 tablespoon **granulated sugar**
¼ teaspoon **ground cinnamon**
⅓ cup **salted butter** at room temperature
½ cup **walnuts**, toasted and chopped (page 104)

Preheat the oven to 375°F. Combine the rhubarb, sugar, and flour in a large bowl. Put the mixture in an unbuttered 2-quart oval baking dish, spreading it out into an even layer.

To make the topping: Combine the flour, sugars, and cinnamon in a large bowl. Work the butter into the dry ingredients with your fingers or a pastry blender until the mixture is crumbly. Add the walnuts and stir to combine. Distribute the mixture evenly over the rhubarb.

Bake for 30 to 45 minutes, or until the topping is golden brown and the rhubarb is tender when pierced with a paring knife. If the topping is brown but the rhubarb is not yet tender, cover the baking dish with aluminum foil and continue to bake another 5 to 10 minutes.

Remove from the oven and let the crisp sit for 10 to 15 minutes before serving. Serve warm.

SPRING VEGETABLES

Chef Tim Rodgers

For those who must endure long winters, spring heralds the long-awaited arrival of fresh vegetables. Asparagus and fiddlehead ferns are two of the first things to pop through the ground. My spring vegetable menu offers great recipes for casual dining, including preparations for asparagus, fiddlehead ferns, portobellos, peas, and strawberries. The salmon-wrapped asparagus is an easy yet impressive way to cook fish. The accompanying chive sauce is simple to prepare.

GRILLED PORTOBELLOS AND FIDDLEHEAD FERNS WITH SPRING GREENS
Serves 8 to 10 as a salad course

DRESSING

5 tablespoons red wine vinegar
2 shallots, minced
1 teaspoon minced garlic
1 teaspoon chopped fresh thyme
1 teaspoon chopped fresh marjoram
1 teaspoon chopped fresh basil
Salt and freshly ground pepper to taste
⅔ cup olive oil

Five 4- to 5-inch-diameter portobello mushrooms, stemmed
2 tablespoons olive oil
½ pound fiddlehead ferns, blanched (page 103), see Chef's Tips
Salt and freshly ground pepper to taste
1 cup croutons (page 104)
10 cups mixed spring greens, rinsed and dried (see Chef's Tips)

To make the dressing: Combine the vinegar, shallots, garlic, thyme, marjoram, basil, salt, and pepper in a large bowl. Gradually whisk in the oil until thoroughly blended. Reserve half the dressing. Toss the portobellos in the remaining dressing and marinate in the refrigerator for 2 hours or overnight.

Preheat a grill to medium heat and oil the rack lightly. Remove the portobellos from the marinade and grill them for 4 to 8 minutes on each side, or until well marked and tender. Let cool slightly before cutting into ¼-inch slices.

Heat the remaining 2 tablespoons of oil in a small sauté pan over high heat. Add the blanched fiddleheads and sauté

(continued on next page)

for about 1 minute, or until heated through. Season with salt and pepper. Add the croutons and toss to coat with oil.

Toss the spring greens with the reserved dressing and divide among chilled salad plates. Divide the mushroom slices among the salads and garnish with fiddleheads and croutons.

Chef's Tips: Fiddlehead ferns are available from April to early July. They should be clear jade green, firm, and no more than about 1 inch across. If fresh fiddleheads are not available, frozen may be used.

Spring greens may include red and green oak leaf lettuces, mâche, mizuna, or Bibb lettuce.

RISOTTO WITH FRESH PEAS AND PANCETTA
Serves 10 as a first course

¼ cup diced pancetta (about 2 ounces)
1 onion, minced
1 cup Arborio rice (see Chef's Tip)
4 cups Chicken Broth (page 107), heated
1 cup fresh green peas, blanched (page 103)
Salt and freshly ground white pepper to taste
1 cup grated Parmesan

Sauté the pancetta in a 2-quart saucepan over medium-high heat until it is golden brown and crisp. Add the onion and sauté until limp, about 3 minutes. Add the rice and stir for 1 to 2 minutes, or until the rice is evenly coated.

Add 1 cup of the heated broth, and cook, stirring constantly, until all the liquid has been absorbed by the rice. Repeat this process 3 more times, or until all of the broth has been added (about 20 to 25 minutes' total cooking time) and the rice is tender. Add the peas and stir for about 2 minutes, or until the peas are warmed through. Season with salt and white pepper.

To serve, ladle the risotto into warmed soup plates and sprinkle with Parmesan and a little more pepper.

Chef's Tip: Arborio is a special Italian rice with plump, round grains that develop a creamy texture but a slightly al dente center when stirred constantly during cooking. Arborio rice can be found in Italian markets or specialty foods stores.

SALMON-WRAPPED ASPARAGUS WITH CHIVE SAUCE
Serves 10 as a main course

3 to 4 bunches asparagus, trimmed to 5 inches
    and blanched (page 103), see Chef's Tip
Ten 6-ounce salmon fillets, skinned
¾ cup dry white wine
¾ cup water
Juice of ½ lemon
2 tablespoons minced shallots
¼ teaspoon salt
¼ teaspoon ground white pepper

CHIVE SAUCE
Reserved poaching liquid from salmon, above
2 tablespoons arrowroot or cornstarch
3 tablespoons dry white wine
¾ cup heavy cream
1 tomato, peeled, seeded, and chopped (page 103)
1 bunch chives, minced
Salt and freshly ground white pepper to taste

Lay bundles of 4 to 10 spears of the blanched asparagus in a baking dish (or dishes). (See Chef's Tip.) Cut each salmon fillet at a 45-degree angle into 3 even pieces and overlap them on an asparagus bundle, leaving the tips uncovered. Tuck the salmon slices under the asparagus so that they are completely wrapped around the bundle. Repeat with the remaining salmon and asparagus.

Preheat the oven to 275°F. Combine the wine, water, lemon juice, and shallots in sauce pot and bring to a very low simmer over medium heat. Gently ladle the poaching liquid over the salmon parcels. Add the salt and pepper, and cover the baking dish(es). Poach in the oven until the salmon is opaque throughout, about 10 minutes. Using a slotted spatula, carefully remove the salmon parcels and keep warm. Pour the poaching liquid into a saucepan to prepare the sauce.

To make the sauce: Place the pan over medium heat and bring the reserved poaching liquid to a simmer. Mix the arrowroot or cornstarch with the wine and whisk into the poaching liquid. Whisk in the heavy cream and cook for 2 minutes, or until the sauce is thickened. Add the tomatoes and chives and season with salt and pepper. Simmer the sauce until all the ingredients are thoroughly heated.

Serve the salmon parcels on warmed plates and spoon the sauce over them.

Chef's Tip: Asparagus spears may be very thin or thick, depending on how early or late in their season you buy them. Adjust the quantity you use for each serving depending on how big the asparagus spears are. You may want only 3 or 4 large asparagus per parcel, or, if they are very thin, as many as 10.

STRAWBERRIES AND SHORTCAKES WITH CLABBERED CREAM
Serves 10

3 pints strawberries, hulled and quartered
3 tablespoons sugar
½ cup fresh orange juice
1 teaspoon minced orange zest (see Chef's Tips)

SHORTCAKES
3 cups all-purpose flour
⅓ cup sugar
1 tablespoon baking powder
1 teaspoon salt
½ cup (1 stick) cold unsalted butter, cut into pieces
¾ cup cold milk

1 egg, beaten
6 ounces (¾ cup) clabbered cream (see Chef's Tips)

Combine the strawberries, sugar, orange juice, and zest in a large bowl. Stir to coat the berries evenly and let them sit at room temperature while making the shortcakes.

To make the shortcakes: Preheat the oven to 375°F. Sift the flour, sugar, baking powder, and salt together into a large bowl. Work in the butter pieces with your fingertips or cut them in with a pastry blender until the mixture is the texture of coarse cornmeal. Make a well in the center and pour in the milk. Mix with a wooden spoon until the mixture pulls away from the side of the bowl.

Roll or pat the dough out on a lightly floured work surface to a thickness of ½ to ¾ inch. It will appear very rough and flaky. Cut out 10 shortcakes with a 3-inch round cutter (see Chef's Tips). Place the shortcakes on an ungreased baking sheet. Brush the tops with the beaten egg. Bake for 15 to 20 minutes, or until the shortcakes just begin to turn golden. Remove from the oven and serve immediately, or let them cool on a wire rack and rewarm in a 250°F oven for 5 minutes just before serving.

To serve, split each shortcake in half and place the bottom piece on a dessert plate. Layer the strawberries with some of their juice and a generous dollop of clabbered cream over the shortcake and finish with the shortcake top over the cream.

Chef's Tips: To make orange zest, use a vegetable peeler to remove just the colored portion of the peel. Mince the peel with a sharp knife.

When cutting out the biscuits, be careful not to twist the cutter or the shortcakes will not rise around the edge.

Clabbered cream is a cultured pasteurized cream available in some specialty foods stores. Lightly whipped unsweetened heavy cream, sour cream, or crème fraîche may also be substituted.

CINCO DE MAYO
SOUTHWESTERN

Chef Bill Phillips

Cinco de Mayo is one of Mexico's most festive holiday, and a fiesta now happily enjoyed throughout the United States as well. It is not Mexico's version of Independence Day, as commonly thought. Instead, it heralds the fortitude of the Mexican people on May 5, 1862, when they successfully held off an invasion of the town of Puebla by the French.

This menu pays homage to the Mexican and Native American influences on the cooking of the Southwest. While relying heavily on a wide range of different fresh and dried chilies, many dishes of the region are, surprisingly, not hot and spicy. They do, however, possess an expansive range of flavors, colors, and textures. The trick is learning how to impart the complex flavors of the chilies without adding too much of their discomforting heat.

BLACK BEAN AND BUTTERNUT SQUASH SOUPS
Serves 6 as a first course

BLACK BEAN SOUP

1 dried chipotle chili, stemmed (page 102)
3 cups cooked black beans (page 103)
1 cup cooking liquid from beans, or water, plus more as needed
¼ teaspoon dried Mexican oregano (page 102)
Optional: ¼ teaspoon chopped dried epazote (page 102)
¼ teaspoon ground cumin
Salt to taste

BUTTERNUT SQUASH SOUP

1 tablespoon butter
2 onions, cut into medium dice
2 carrots, cut into medium dice
3 small butternut squash, cut into medium dice (about 4 cups)
¼ cup honey
¼ teaspoon ground cinnamon
⅛ teaspoon ground allspice
Salt to taste

To make the black bean soup: Grind the chipotle chili into a powder in a spice grinder.

Purée the ground chipotle, beans, liquid or water, oregano, epazote, and cumin in a blender until smooth. Thin the soup with a little additional bean liquid or water if necessary. Bring the soup to a boil in a medium saucepan over medium heat. Season with salt. Reduce the heat to low and keep the soup hot until ready to serve. (See Chef's Tip.)

To make the butternut squash soup: Melt the butter in a large saucepan over medium-low heat. Add the onions and carrots and sauté until the onions are tender, about 7 to 10 minutes. Add the squash and enough water to cover the vegetables by about 3 inches. Simmer, uncovered, until the squash and carrots are fork tender, about 30 minutes. Stir in the honey, cinnamon and allspice and simmer 2 minutes longer. Remove the soup from the heat and let cool for 10 minutes.

Purée the soup in a blender until smooth. (Thin the soup with a little water if necessary.) Pour the soup back into saucepan and bring it to a simmer over medium heat. Season with salt. Reduce heat to low and keep the soup hot until ready to serve. (See Chef's Tip.)

To serve: Simultaneously ladle equal amounts of the soups side by side into warmed soup bowls or plates. Swirl the two soups together with a toothpick. Serve at once.

Chef's Tip: The two separate soups may be prepared a day or two ahead of time. Let them cool to room temperature, then cover and refrigerate for up to 2 days. When you are ready to serve them bring them slowly to a simmer over low heat, stirring frequently.

PUEBLO GRILLED CHICKEN AND MANGO QUESADILLAS
Serves 6 as an appetizer

2 pasilla chilies, seeded (page 102
2 guajillo chilies, seeded (page 102)
1 ancho chili, seeded (page 102)
2 tablespoons ground coriander
1 tablespoon ground cumin
1½ teaspoons dried Mexican oregano (page 102)
1 teaspoon ground cinnamon
½ teaspoon ground allspice
1¼ teaspoons salt, plus more to taste
4 boneless, skinless chicken breast halves
½ cup vegetable oil, or as needed
Freshly ground pepper to taste
Six 12-inch flour tortillas
1½ cups grated Monterey Jack cheese
2 mangos, peeled, flesh cut away from the pit, and cut into small dice (see Chef's Tips)

Preheat a grill to high heat. Grind the chilies to a powder in a spice grinder or coffee mill. Combine the powdered chilies, coriander, cumin, oregano, cinnamon, allspice, and the 1¼ teaspoons salt in a large bowl. Mix well and set aside.

Brush the chicken with 2 tablespoons of the oil. Season with salt and pepper. Grill the chicken for 3 minutes on the first side, then turn and grill for 2 minutes on the second side, or until opaque throughout. Remove the chicken from the grill and let cool to room temperature. Shred the chicken into ⅛-inch pieces and toss them in the spice mixture.

Heat 3 tablespoons of the oil in a large sauté pan over medium heat and sauté the chicken mixture just long enough to toast the spices and blend the flavors, about 4 minutes. Be careful not to blacken the spices.

(continued on next page)

To assemble the quesadillas: Lay out 3 tortillas on a work surface and layer them with one half of the cheese, all of the chicken mixture, all of the diced mangos, and finally the remaining cheese. The filling should completely cover the surface of the tortillas. Place a second tortilla over each stack and press down lightly to seal. (If making the quesadillas ahead, cover with plastic wrap and refrigerate for up to 3 hours.)

Heat 1 tablespoon of the oil in a large sauté pan over medium heat. Place 1 quesadilla in the pan and cook until golden brown on the bottom, about 4 minutes. Carefully turn the quesadilla over and brown the other side, about 4 more minutes. Transfer from the pan to a cutting board. Cut into 8 wedges. Repeat to cook the remaining quesadillas, adding 1 tablespoon oil each time. Keep the finished quesadillas warm in a 200°F oven while preparing the remaining quesadillas. Serve 4 wedges per person.

Chef's Tip: Other fruits, such as plums or peaches, may be used in place of the mangos.

PAN-SEARED CORIANDER-CRUSTED SALMON WITH CARAMELIZED RED ONIONS WITH RED AND YELLOW PEPPER COULIS
Serve 6 as a main course

CARAMELIZED RED ONIONS
 3 tablespoons olive oil
 5 red onions, cut into ½-inch-thick slices

CORIANDER-CRUSTED SALMON
 6 tablespoons coriander seeds
 2 teaspoons black peppercorns
 Six 6-ounce salmon fillets, skinned
 ½ teaspoon salt
 5 tablespoons olive oil

Red and Yellow Pepper Coulis (recipe follows)
Green Chili Rice (recipe follows)
6 teaspoons black sesame seeds for garnish
  (see Chef's Tip)

To make the caramelized onions: Heat the oil in a large sauté pan over medium heat. Add the onions in batches and cook, turning occasionally, for about 20 minutes, or until a deep brown color on both sides. Set aside and keep warm.

To prepare the salmon: Preheat the oven to 350°F. Grind the coriander seeds and peppercorns coarsely in a mini chopper or spice grinder. Season the salmon fillets with salt, then coat one side of the fillets with the spice mixture, pressing firmly to adhere.

Preheat the oven to 350°F. Heat the olive oil in a large ovenproof sauté pan over medium-high heat. Place the salmon fillets, spice-side down, in the pan and sear lightly, about 2 minutes. Turn the fillets over and transfer the pan to the oven. Bake the salmon until opaque throughout, about 7 minutes. Remove from the oven and keep warm.

To serve, alternate pools of warmed red and yellow pepper coulis on warmed plates. Shake each plate gently so the sauces run together slightly. Make a bed of rice and caramelized onions on each plate and top with a salmon fillet, crust-side up. Sprinkle with sesame seeds for garnish.

Chef's Tip: Black sesame seeds are available at Asian foods stores.

RED AND YELLOW PEPPER COULIS
Serves 6; makes about 3 cups

5 red peppers, seeded, deribbed, and halved
1 teaspoon sugar
½ teaspoon salt
5 yellow peppers, seeded, deribbed, and halved

Put the red peppers in a large saucepan. Add water to cover the peppers halfway. Cover the pot and cook the peppers over medium heat for 20 minutes. Put the peppers and their cooking liquid in a blender with ½ teaspoon of the sugar and ¼ teaspoon of the salt. Purée until smooth. Let cool.

Repeat the process with the yellow peppers. Cover and refrigerate the sauces separately until needed. To serve, reheat the sauces separately over medium heat and serve warm.

Chef's Tip: The sauces may be stored up to 2 days in the refrigerator.

GREEN CHILI RICE
Serve 6 as a side dish

8 poblano chilies, roasted, peeled,
   and seeded (page 104)
½ cup chopped fresh basil
½ cup chopped fresh cilantro
Leaves from 2 marjoram sprigs, chopped
3½ cups water
5 tablespoons butter
2 garlic cloves, minced
2 cups long-grain white rice
1¼ teaspoons salt

Preheat the oven to 350°F. Combine the chilies, basil, cilantro, marjoram, and water in a blender or food processor and purée until smooth.

Melt the butter in a large ovenproof saucepan over medium heat. Add the garlic and stir for 1 minute, or just until the aroma is released. Add the rice and stir for 1 minute. Add the chili purée and salt. Bring to a boil, cover, and place in the oven for 18 to 20 minutes, or until the rice is tender. Remove the saucepan from the oven and fluff the rice gently with a fork.

CINCO DE MAYO
MEXICAN

Chef Bill Phillips

Mexican cuisine is a blend of Spanish, Aztec, and Mayan techniques and ingredients.

Tamales are a mixture of flavorful ingredients encased in cornmeal dough, or masa. This stiff dough was traditionally made by hand, but the modern food processor has simplified this arduous task. Two types of tamales prevail throughout Mexico: masa wrapped in corn husks and masa wrapped in banana leaves.

Snapper is a fish readily available in Mexico. I serve it here with one of my favorite moles, manchamantel sauce, which literally means "tablecloth stainer."

PORK AND RED CHILI TAMALES IN BANANA LEAVES
Serves 6 as an appetizer

SHREDDED PORK FILLING
1 pound boneless pork loin, cut into 1-inch pieces
1 onion, peeled and left whole
1 teaspoon minced garlic
4 cups water

RED CHILI SAUCE
2 tablespoons olive oil
1 onion, cut into small dice
1 dried chipotle chili, stemmed and seeded (page 102)
1 ancho chili, stemmed and seeded (page 102)
5 garlic cloves, minced
1 plum tomato, chopped
1 cup water
1 tablespoon raisins
1 tablespoon whole almonds, toasted (page 104)
¼ teaspoon ground cinnamon
⅛ teaspoon ground allspice
1 clove
⅛ teaspoon dried Mexican oregano (page 102)
Salt to taste

MASA DOUGH
1½ cups masa harina (page 102)
Salt to taste
3 tablespoons lard, plus as needed for banana leaves
2 cups reserved pork broth from shredded pork, above

6 large banana leaves (page 102)

To make the filling: Combine the pork, onion, garlic, and water in a large saucepan. Bring to a boil, reduce heat to a simmer, and cook for 45 minutes, or until tender. Drain the meat, reserving the cooking liquid. Remove and discard the onion. Finely shred the meat and set aside.

To make the sauce: Heat the olive oil in a large, heavy saucepan over medium-high heat. Add the diced onion and cook, stirring frequently, for 15 minutes, or until light golden brown. Add the chilies and garlic. Stir for 1 minute to toast the chilies. Add the tomato, water, raisins, almonds, spices, and oregano and simmer for 15 minutes, stirring occasionally. Transfer to a blender and purée until smooth. Season with salt.

Pour the puréed sauce back into the saucepan and add the shredded pork. Simmer until the sauce is thickened, about 5 minutes.

To make the masa dough: Using a food processor, electric mixer fitted with a paddle attachment, or a wooden spoon, beat the masa harina, salt, and lard until the dough comes together. Add the pork broth and continue beating until the mixture is light and spongy, about 5 minutes. Cover and refrigerate for 20 minutes. Form into balls 1¼ inches in diameter.

To make the tamales: Heat 3 of the banana leaves over a gas burner or under a broiler until they soften and become pliable. Cut the leaves into six 8-inch squares. Lightly grease one side of the squares with lard and place a ball of masa on each square. Flatten the dough with the palm of your hand to a ¼-inch thickness. Top the masa with 1½ tablespoons of the pork filling. Fold the edges of each banana leaf toward the center and the top and bottom over to form a square package.

Place the remaining banana leaves in the bottom of a large steamer, folding them to fit, if necessary. Cover them with water and bring the water to a slow boil. Arrange the tamales in the top of the steamer, seam-side down. Cover and steam until cooked through, about 45 minutes. Unwrap the tamales from the banana leaves and serve. (Do not eat the banana leaves.)

GRILLED RED SNAPPER AND MARINATED JÍCAMA WITH MANCHAMANTEL SAUCE

MARINATED JÍCAMA
1 jícama, peeled and cut into julienne
1 cup fresh lime juice
¼ cup chopped fresh cilantro
Salt to taste

Six 6-ounce red snapper fillets, skin on
¼ cup olive oil, or as needed
Salt and freshly ground pepper to taste
4 cups Manchamantel Sauce (recipe follows)
Black Rice (recipe follows)

To make the marinated jícama: Combine all the ingredients for the marinated jícama in a medium bowl and toss to coat the jícama. Refrigerate for 1 hour.

Preheat a grill to medium-high heat. Dip the fillets in the olive oil and let the excess oil drain off. Season on both sides with salt and pepper. Grill the snapper, skin-side down, for 4 minutes. Turn the fish once and grill for 3 minutes, or until just opaque throughout. Transfer the fillets to warmed plates, skin-side up. Serve each fillet at once with the manchamantel sauce, marinated jícama, and black rice.

MANCHAMANTEL SAUCE
Serves 6; makes about 6 cups

5 ancho chilies (page 102)
3 guajillo chilies (page 102)
2 tablespoons olive oil
1 onion, cut into medium dice
3 garlic cloves, minced
½ pineapple, peeled and cored
3 plum tomatoes
2 Granny Smith, or other tart green apples,
    peeled and cored
2 pears, peeled and cored
2 peaches, pitted and peeled
1 tablespoon fresh lime juice
1 tablespoon sugar
2 teaspoons salt
1½ teaspoons ground cinnamon
¼ teaspoon ground allspice
⅛ teaspoon ground cloves

Preheat the oven to 250°F. Spread the chilies on a baking sheet and heat them in the oven for 1½ minutes. Remove from the oven and seed the chilies. Put the chilies in a medium saucepan and add water to cover. Bring to a boil, reduce heat to a simmer, cover and cook for 15 minutes. Using a slotted spoon, remove the chilies from the cooking liquid and set aside. Reserve the cooking liquid.

Heat the oil in a small sauté pan over medium heat. Add the onion and sauté until golden, about 12 to 15 minutes. Add the garlic and sauté for 1 minute.

Combine the chilies, onion mixture, and all the remaining ingredients in a large bowl and toss until combined. Place the mixture in a blender in batches and purée to make a smooth sauce.

Place the sauce in a medium saucepan and bring it to a simmer over medium heat. Thin the sauce with a little of the reserved cooking liquid from the chilies, if necessary. If the sauce is too thin, simmer over medium heat until it is thick enough to coat the back of a wooden spoon. Serve the sauce warm.

Chef's Tip: The amount of sauce you will get from this recipe may vary, depending on the sizes of the fruits and tomatoes. If you have more than you need for the red snapper recipe, let the remainder cool, cover, and store in the refrigerator for up to 3 days. Serve the leftover sauce with grilled or roasted pork or chicken.

BLACK RICE
Serves 6 as a side dish

1 cup cooked black beans (page 103)
2½ cups cooking liquid from beans,
    and/or water as needed
1 tablespoon ground cumin
Salt to taste
5 tablespoons butter
2 cups long-grain white rice

Preheat the oven to 350°F. Purée the beans in a blender with the cooking liquid or water, cumin, and salt until smooth. Add a little water if necessary to thin.

Melt the butter in a large, heavy ovenproof saucepan over medium heat. Add the rice and stir for 1 minute. Add the bean purée. Taste and adjust the seasoning, if necessary. Bring to a boil and cover the pan. Bake the rice for 18 to 20 minutes, or until it is tender. Remove the pan from the oven and fluff the rice gently with a fork.

Strawberries and Shortcakes with Clabbered Cream
Page 25

Smoked Shrimp with Sauce Lamaze
Page 79

Rosemary-Skewered Chicken and Mushroom Kabobs with Grilled Flatbread
Page 60

Cheese Sticks, Parmesan Crisps, Spiced Mixed Nuts and Candied Nuts
Page 45 and Page 46

Bread Salad Tuscan Style
Page14

Risotto with Fresh Peas and Pancetta
Page 24

Black Bean and Butternut Squash Soups
Page 26

Smoked Salmon and Smashed-Potato Pancakes
Page 41

COOKING FOR MOM

Chef Bill Reynolds

Taking mom out to a restaurant for dinner on Mother's Day is a wonderful tradition, but that doesn't mean you can't cook her a special breakfast or brunch earlier in the day. This menu features some fine opportunities to indulge your mother and show off your talents.

Smoked salmon and "smashed" potatoes gives a new twist to the traditional potato pancake. A chef's skill is often judged by his or her ability to make a perfect omelet. You'll be cooking (and looking) like a pro with this cheese omelet topped with asparagus sauce accompanied with your own homemade sausage. The Dutch baby with spiced fruit can be made as one large family-style serving or as individual servings.

SMOKED SALMON AND SMASHED-POTATO PANCAKES
Serves 6 as a first course

12 slices smoked salmon
1 bunch leeks, white part only,
    cut into fine julienne (page 103)
2 cups olive oil
6 Red Bliss potatoes (about 2 inches in diameter)
Salt and freshly ground pepper to taste
3 tablespoons vegetable oil (see Chef's Tip)
6 tablespoons sour cream
6 tablespoons Herbed Oil (page 106)
2 tablespoons capers, drained
6 tablespoons salmon caviar

Overlap 2 of the salmon slices and roll them up to resemble a rose. Repeat with the remaining salmon slices. Refrigerate until needed.

Combine the leeks and olive oil in a large, heavy saucepan. Place the pan over medium heat. After about 5 minutes, the leeks will rise to the surface. Cook for 5 minutes longer, stirring occasionally, or until the leeks are golden but still soft. (They will crisp as they cool.) Using a slotted spoon, transfer the leeks to paper towels to drain. Separate the leeks so they don't stick together.

Put the potatoes in a medium saucepan and add cold water to cover. Add a little salt and bring to a simmer over medium-high heat. Cook for 10 to 15 minutes, or until the potatoes are tender when pierced with the tip of a paring knife. The skins should still be intact.

Drain the potatoes and pat them dry with paper towels. While the potatoes are still quite warm, place them between 2 pieces of waxed paper and smash them with the smooth side of a mallet or the bottom of a heavy pan. Season with salt and pepper on both sides. Heat the vegetable oil in a large

(continued on next page)

sauté pan over medium-high heat. Using a metal spatula, transfer the smashed potatoes to the pan and fry for 5 minutes on the first side, or until brown and crisp. Turn and fry for 2 minutes on the second side, or until brown and crisp.

To serve, mound the leeks in the center of a warmed serving platter or individual plates and arrange the potatoes on top of the leeks. Top each potato with a dollop of sour cream and a salmon "rose." Garnish with the herbed oil, capers, and salmon caviar. Serve while the potatoes are warm.

Chef's Tip: For a little extra flavor, replace half of the vegetable oil with clarified butter (page 104).

DUTCH BABY WITH SPICED FRUIT
Serves 6 as a brunch dish

½ cup all-purpose flour
½ teaspoon salt
2 eggs, well beaten
½ cup milk
4 tablespoons (½ stick) unsalted butter, melted
1 tablespoon fresh lemon juice
3 peaches, peeled and sliced
2 tablespoons ground cinnamon
2 tablespoons firmly packed brown sugar
Powdered sugar as needed
1½ tablespoons heavy cream, whipped to soft peaks
1 teaspoon grated lemon zest

Preheat the oven to 450°F. Sift the flour and salt together into a small bowl.

Put the eggs in a blender and blend at low speed. Add the flour mixture and the milk alternately, in thirds. Scrape down the sides of the blender and continue to blend until smooth. Blend in 2 tablespoons of the melted butter. Pour the batter into a nonstick or well-greased 10-inch cast-iron skillet or ovenproof sauté pan. Bake for 20 minutes without

opening the oven door. Reduce the heat to 350°F and bake 10 minutes longer.

While the Dutch baby is baking, prepare the spiced fruit: Heat the remaining 2 tablespoons melted butter in a medium sauté pan over high heat. Add the peaches, cinnamon, and brown sugar. Reduce heat to medium and stir until the fruit is just heated through, about 5 minutes.

Remove the Dutch baby from the oven and transfer to a warm serving plate. Drizzle with the lemon juice and sprinkle with the powdered sugar. Fill the center of the Dutch baby with the hot fruit mixture. Top with the whipped cream and lemon zest. Serve at once.

Chef's Tips: Substitute sour cream or yogurt for the whipped cream, if you prefer.

For the spiced fruit, substitute other fruits, or combinations of fruits such as bananas, raspberries, apples, and/or strawberries, if you like.

CHEESE OMELETS WITH ASPARAGUS SAUCE
Serves 6

ASPARAGUS SAUCE
  12 to 18 asparagus spears
  2 tablespoons unsalted butter
  2 tablespoons all-purpose flour
  2 cups Chicken Broth (page 107)
  Salt and freshly ground pepper to taste

CHEESE OMELETS
  12 eggs
  ¾ cup water
  Salt and freshly ground white pepper to taste
  ½ cup vegetable oil, or clarified butter (page 104),
    as needed
  1½ cups grated Cheddar, Swiss,
    and/or Monterey Jack cheese

To make the sauce: Trim and discard the bottom inch of the asparagus. Peel the asparagus stalks and cut them into 2-inch pieces. Set aside, reserving the tips separately for garnish.

Heat the butter in a 2-quart saucepan over medium heat. Add the flour and stir well with a wooden spoon. Reduce the heat to low and cook, stirring frequently, for 5 minutes, or until the mixture has a pleasant "nutty" aroma, but do not allow it to brown. Whisk in the broth to make a smooth sauce. Add the asparagus stalks, bring the sauce to a gentle simmer, and cook for 30 minutes. Purée the sauce in a blender or food processor. Strain through a sieve and season with salt and pepper. (See Chef's Tip.) Keep warm.

Cook the asparagus tips in salted boiling water for 3 to 5 minutes, or until barely tender. Drain at once and rinse with cold water to stop the cooking. Set aside. Just before cooking the omelets, add the tips to the sauce and warm over low heat for 3 to 5 minutes.

To make each omelet: Beat 2 eggs and 1 tablespoon of water together in a small bowl until thoroughly blended. Add salt and white pepper. Heat enough oil or clarified butter to generously coat a 6-inch omelet pan over medium heat (use less for a nonstick pan, more for regular pan). Pour in the eggs. Simultaneously stir the eggs with one hand and shake the pan back and forth on the burner with the other. When the eggs are almost set, place ¼ cup of the cheese in a line down the center of the omelet. Roll the omelet out of the pan and onto a warmed serving plate. Top with some of the sauce and asparagus tips and serve at once. Repeat the process to make the remaining omelets.

Chef's Tip: This sauce is referred to as a velouté *in professional kitchens. It may be made a day or two in advance. If you make the sauce ahead of time, pour it into a clean bowl, let cool to room temperature, cover, and refrigerate. To reheat the sauce, bring it to a simmer over medium heat, stirring frequently. Taste and adjust the seasoning, if necessary.*

HOMEMADE BREAKFAST
SAUSAGE LINKS OR PATTIES
Makes about 25 patties or links

4 pounds boneless pork butt, cut into ½-inch pieces
¾ cup ice water
1 tablespoon poultry seasoning
2 tablespoons salt, plus more if needed
2 teaspoons ground pepper, plus more if needed
Vegetable oil for sautéing

Combine the meat, ice water, poultry seasoning, 2 table-spoons salt, and 2 teaspoons pepper in a large bowl. Grind the meat once through the grinding plate (⅛-inch holes) of a meat grinder. Or, place half of the mixture in a food processor and pulse for 1 minute to make sure the meat and fat are ground together evenly; repeat with the remaining meat mixture.

Bring a small saucepan of water to a simmer over medium heat. Form a spoonful of the sausage mixture into a small dumpling and poach it in the water for 2 minutes. Taste the cooked dumpling and adjust the seasoning of the remaining sausage mixture, if necessary. The sausage mixture is now ready to be formed into links or patties.

To make patties: Form the meat mixture into a cylinder about 2½ inches in diameter. Wrap the cylinder in plastic wrap. Secure the ends of the plastic tightly with twist ties or strings. Refrigerate the sausage roll for at least 1 hour to firm it up. Unwrap the cylinder and cut it into ½-inch-thick patties as needed. Sauté them in a little oil over medium heat until browned, about 5 to 8 minutes on each side.

To make links: Fill a pastry bag without a tip with the sausage mixture. Cut a sheet of plastic wrap about 3 feet long. Pipe out a continuous line of meat mixture, about ¾ inch in diameter, along the long side of the plastic wrap. Roll the sausage mixture up tightly and tie one end of the plastic wrap with string. Use string to tie off links every 3 inches. Tie the other end of the plastic tightly. Poke the plastic wrap surrounding each link with a toothpick to release any air bubbles. Repeat with the remaining sausage.

Bring a large pot of water to a low simmer. Poach the entire strand of links for 15 to 20 minutes, or until one link registers an internal temperature of 165°F on an instant-read thermometer. Let the links cool. Remove the plastic wrap.

To brown the sausage links, heat a little oil in a sauté pan over medium heat. Cook the links, turning frequently, until evenly browned, about 5 to 8 minutes. Transfer to paper towels to drain briefly before serving.

Chef's Tips: Links and patties may be stored in their plastic wrap for up to 3 days in the refrigerator or up to 1 month in the freezer.

The ice water may have some small pieces of ice in it. Pulse the meat and ice water mixture quickly; don't overdo the processing, or the fat and meat will separate.

PARTY BUFFET

Chef Tim Rodgers

The month of May marks the beginning of party season. Spring is well underway and welcomes the celebrations of graduations, weddings, and christenings. A buffet is one of the easier ways to serve a group of people and affords the opportunity to try out some new recipes. My party buffet menu offers candied and spiced nuts, cheese crisps and sticks, and home-cured salmon (gravlax). I'll show you how easy it is to smoke-roast a tenderloin of beef. To make it even easier on yourself, let your guests slice off pieces for themselves. These simple yet elegant finger foods are sure to make the party a success.

CHEESE STICKS
PAILLETTES
Makes about 24 sticks

1 sheet puff pastry, thawed
1 egg yolk
2 tablespoons milk
¼ teaspoon salt
½ cup grated Parmesan
Paprika for dusting

Preheat the oven to 400°F. On a lightly floured work surface, roll the puff pastry out into a rectangle about 12-by-18 inches and ⅛-inch thickness. Beat the egg yolk, milk, and salt together in a small bowl. Brush the puff pastry with the egg mixture. Sprinkle the Parmesan evenly over the puff pastry. Dust lightly with paprika. Cut crosswise into ½-inch-wide strips. Twist each strip 5 or 6 times to form a spiral and place on a baking sheet. Bake the strips for 15 minutes, or until golden brown. Serve warm or at room temperature.

Chef's Tip: Store in an airtight container in a cool, dry place for 2 to 3 days. Do not refrigerate the baked sticks or they will lose their crispness.

PARMESAN CRISPS
Makes about 24 crisps

1 pound Parmesan in a block

Preheat the oven to 350°F. Using a box grater, cut the cheese into small shreds, making the strands as long as possible. On a nonstick or well-greased baking sheet, sprinkle the cheese in 3-inch circles about ¼ inch thick. Bake until just melted and golden brown, about 7 to 10 minutes. Remove with a thin metal spatula (see Chef's Tips) and let cool.

(continued on next page)

Chef's Tips: While still warm, the crisps may be molded into various shapes. Try placing them over a rolling pin to make a saddle or over a small bowl to make a cup.

Store in an airtight container in a cool, dry place for 2 to 3 days. Do not refrigerate the crisps or they will wilt.

Aged goat cheese, dry Jack, or romano cheese may be used in place of Parmesan.

SPICED MIXED NUTS
Makes 2 cups

2 tablespoons unsalted butter
1 tablespoon Worcestershire sauce
2 cups unsalted raw whole mixed nuts
½ teaspoon celery seed
½ teaspoon garlic powder
½ teaspoon chili powder
½ teaspoon salt
¼ teaspoon ground cumin
⅛ teaspoon cayenne pepper

Preheat the oven to 375°F. Melt the butter over medium heat in a medium sauté pan. Add the Worcestershire sauce and bring to a simmer. Add the nuts and toss well to coat evenly. Sprinkle the spices and salt over the nuts and toss well to coat evenly, about 2 minutes.

Place the nuts on a nonstick or well-greased baking sheet and bake, stirring occasionally, for 10 to 12 minutes, or until evenly browned. Let cool completely before serving.

Chef's Tips: If saltier nuts are desired, sprinkle with kosher salt while still warm.

Store in an airtight container in a cool, dry place for up to 10 days.

CANDIED NUTS
Makes 2 cups

1 egg white
2 tablespoons water
2 cups (10 ounces) whole pecans or walnuts
½ cup superfine sugar
1 teaspoon salt
2 teaspoons ground cinnamon
1 teaspoon ground ginger
1 teaspoon ground cardamom
¾ teaspoon ground allspice
½ teaspoon ground coriander
Pinch cayenne pepper

Preheat the oven to 250°F. Combine the egg white and water in a large bowl and beat until lightly frothy. Add the nuts and stir until completely coated. Drain well in a colander.

Combine the sugar, salt, and spices in a medium plastic or paper bag and shake to blend. Transfer the nuts to the bag and shake until the nuts are completely coated. Turn the nuts out on a baking sheet and spread out in a single layer. Bake for about 10 minutes, then lower the oven temperature to 225°F and bake, stirring occasionally, for another 10 minutes, or until the nuts are dark golden brown. Let cool completely before serving.

Chef's Tip: Store in an airtight container in a cool, dry place for up to 10 days.

GRAVLAX
Serves 12 to 14 as an appetizer

Gravlax is not difficult to make at home, although it does require 3 days to properly cure. For variations on home-cured salmon, see the Chef's Tips.

CURE
  2 cups sugar
  1 cup kosher salt
  2 tablespoons cracked pepper

  One 3-to 4-pound salmon fillet, skin on
  Juice of 1 lemon
  Leaves from 2 dill bunches, chopped

GARNISH
  1 loaf rye bread, cut into triangles
  3 hard-cooked eggs, yolks and whites separated
    and finely chopped or sieved
  3 tablespoons capers, drained and rinsed
  ½ red onion, minced, rinsed, and drained

To make the cure: Combine all the cure ingredients in a large bowl and mix thoroughly.

Place the salmon fillet, skin-side down, on a 2-foot piece of plastic wrap. Sprinkle the fillet with the lemon juice. Cover the fillet evenly with the cure. Sprinkle the dill evenly over the cure. Wrap the sides of the plastic wrap over the salmon, leaving the ends open. Prick the sides, top, and bottom of the plastic. (This allows the juices to seep out.)

Place the wrapped fillet in a shallow pan. Top with another pan containing a 2- to 3-pound weight. Let rest in the refrigerator for 3 days, turning once after 36 hours. Remove the fillet and scrape off the cure.

To serve, slice the gravlax very thinly starting at the tail, cutting at a 45-degree angle. Arrange the gravlax on a platter and serve with the rye bread triangles and side dishes of egg yolks, egg whites, capers, and red onion, to be added by your guests.

Chef's Tips: Try the following variations: Replace the lemon juice with lime juice and the dill with cilantro.

Replace the salt and pepper in the cure with either a Cajun or a Southwestern spice mix.

SMOKE-ROASTED TENDERLOIN OF BEEF WITH HORSERADISH-MUSTARD SAUCE
Serves 10 to 12 as an appetizer

For the best flavor, allow at least 1 full day for the beef to marinate.

MARINADE
  ¼ cup vegetable oil
  3 garlic cloves, minced
  1 tablespoon chopped fresh rosemary
  1 tablespoon chopped fresh thyme
  1 tablespoon cracked pepper
  2 teaspoons salt

  1 trimmed beef tenderloin piece (about 3 pounds),
    tied with butcher's twine
  1 cup hickory wood chips
  Horseradish-Mustard Sauce (recipe follows)
  French bread for serving

To make the marinade: Combine all the marinade ingredients in a bowl. Place the tenderloin in shallow pan. Brush the tenderloin with marinade, making sure all the herbs are evenly distributed. Cover with plastic wrap and refrigerate for at least 24 or up to 48 hours.

Preheat a grill to high heat. Grill the meat over high heat until seared on all sides, about 5 to 8 minutes. Place on a wire rack.

(continued on next page)

Make a small tray out of aluminum foil and add the wood chips. Place the pan of chips directly over the heating element or the hottest area of the coals. When the chips start to smoke, place the tenderloin on the cooking rack. Cover the grill and smoke-roast for a total 20 to 30 minutes for medium-rare; adjust the cooking time to achieve the doneness you prefer. Let the meat rest 10 minutes before carving.

To serve, cut into thin slices and serve with the horseradish-mustard sauce and slices of French bread.

Chef's Tip: Ask your butcher to tie the tenderloin for you.

HORSERADISH-MUSTARD SAUCE
Makes 1½ cups

1 cup mayonnaise
¼ cup prepared horseradish
1 tablespoon Dijon mustard
Salt and freshly ground pepper to taste
1 teaspoon fresh lemon juice
Tabasco sauce to taste

Combine all the ingredients in a medium bowl and stir until well blended. Refrigerate until needed.

Chef's Tip: Cover and store in the refrigerator for up to 3 days.

MEMORIAL BARBECUE AT ITS BEST

Chef Bob Briggs

Memorial Day truly marks the beginning of summer and ushers in the season of cooking out of doors. My menu is built on a repertoire of all-American standards. These classics have been modified so that they now hold special meaning for me and my family. The barbecued spareribs are a particular favorite of my daughter Ashley, while the Boston baked beans are mine, a version of those my mother made every Saturday while I was growing up in New Hampshire. The flavor and texture of roasted corn, along with Cheddar cheese, make for a unique corn bread. Other Briggs family originals are the pasta salad and cole slaw. The pasta salad has plenty of vegetables and no mayonnaise, while the cole slaw stands apart from others with a tangy taste from the sour cream and mustard.

CORN BREAD WITH CHEDDAR CHEESE AND ROASTED CORN
Serves 8

1 teaspoon shortening or lard
¾ cup all-purpose flour
⅓ cup sugar
2 teaspoons baking powder
1 teaspoon salt
1 cup cornmeal
2 eggs
1 cup milk or buttermilk
½ cup (1 stick) unsalted butter, melted
½ cup grated sharp Cheddar cheese
Kernels cut from 2 ears roasted corn (see Chef's Tip)

Preheat a grill to high heat. Coat the inside of an 8-inch round cake pan, cast-iron skillet, or corn-stick pan with the shortening or lard. Place the greased pan on the grill and cover the grill to preheat the pan, for 10 minutes while mixing the corn bread.

Sift the flour, sugar, baking powder, and salt together into a large bowl. Stir in the cornmeal until well blended.

Combine the eggs, milk or buttermilk, and melted butter in a small bowl and beat until blended. Pour the wet ingredients into the dry ingredients and mix lightly with a wooden spoon or a rubber spatula just until a moist batter is formed. Gently fold in the Cheddar cheese and corn kernels.

Pour the mixture into the preheated pan and place it on the grill. Cover the grill and bake for 15 to 20 minutes, or until the bread is brown and starts to pull away from the sides of the pan. Let cool slightly before serving directly from the pan.

Chef's Tips: To roast corn, trim the stem and loose silk off the ends of the ears of corn, leaving the husks on. Place the corn on the grill, cover the grill, and roast until tender, about 30 to 40

(continued on next page)

minutes. Give the corn a quarter turn every 5 minutes. The husks should blacken, but be careful not to burn the kernels. Remove the corn from the grill and let it to cool to the touch. Pull off the husks and any remaining silk, and cut the kernels from the cob.

This recipe may be made with 1 to 1½ cups thawed frozen corn kernels as a substitute for the roasted corn.

The corn bread may be baked in a preheated 375°F oven for 15 to 20 minutes.

BARBECUED SPARERIBS
Serves 8 as a main course

MARINADE
1 cup apple cider vinegar
1 cup apple cider or apple juice
¼ cup Worcestershire sauce
¼ cup lightly packed brown sugar
4 garlic cloves, minced
2 teaspoons Tabasco sauce, or to taste
2 tablespoons salt

3 pounds spareribs, trimmed and silverskin removed
   (see Chef's Tip)
Barbecue Sauce (recipe follows)

To make the marinade: Combine all the marinade ingredients in a medium mixing bowl and whisk to blend. Place the ribs and the marinade in a large, heavy self-sealing plastic bag, seal, and refrigerate overnight.

The next day, drain and rinse the ribs. Pat them dry with paper towels and allow to dry thoroughly on a rack before grilling.

Preheat a grill to a low heat. Grill the ribs, covered, for 30 minutes, turning every 5 minutes. Brush on an even layer of barbecue sauce and grill, covered, for 20 minutes longer, basting with additional sauce every few minutes, until ribs are well glazed.

Remove the ribs from the grill and cut between each rib bone to serve. Pass any remaining barbecue sauce on the side.

Chef's Tip: Silverskin is a tough whitish membrane on the inside of the ribs. Loosen it with the tip of a boning or paring knife and pull and cut it away before marinating the ribs.

BARBECUE SAUCE
Makes 4 cups

2 tablespoons vegetable oil
1 onion, cut into small dice
2 tablespoons minced garlic
¼ cup chili powder
2 tablespoons minced jalapeño chili,
   or to taste (see Chef's Tip)
1 cup tomato paste
1 cup brewed coffee
1 cup Worcestershire sauce
½ cup apple cider vinegar
½ cup lightly packed brown sugar
½ cup apple cider or apple juice

Heat the vegetable oil in a heavy 2-quart saucepan over medium heat. Add the onion and garlic and sauté until translucent, about 3 minutes. Add the chili powder and jalapeño. Sauté for 1 minute. Add the tomato paste and cook, stirring constantly, for 2 minutes. Add all the remaining ingredients and simmer for 10 to 15 minutes, stirring occasionally. Use immediately, or let cool to room temperature before storing in a clean, covered container in the refrigerator. It will keep for up to 1 month.

Chef's Tip: If a milder sauce is preferred, omit the jalapeño.

BOSTON BAKED BEANS
Serves 8 as a side dish

1 onion, cut into medium dice
3 garlic cloves, minced
2 cups dried pea beans or navy beans,
  soaked and drained (page 102)
2 cups water
⅓ cup molasses
¼ cup lightly packed brown sugar
¼ cup medium dice sun-dried tomatoes
  (see Chef's Tip)
1 tablespoon dry mustard
1 bay leaf
½ teaspoon salt
¼ teaspoon cracked pepper
One 3-ounce chunk salt pork, or 4 slices bacon
⅓ cup ketchup
2 tablespoons apple cider vinegar

Preheat the oven to 300°F. Spread the onion and garlic in the bottom of a 1½-quart ceramic bean pot or ovenproof pot with a tight-fitting lid. Top with the beans.

Combine the water, molasses, brown sugar, sun-dried tomatoes, mustard, bay leaf, salt, and pepper in a medium saucepan and bring to a boil over high heat. Reduce heat to a simmer and cook for 2 minutes. Pour the mixture over the beans.

Slice the salt pork from the fat side almost to, but not through, the skin. Place the salt pork, skin-side up, on top of the beans. If using bacon, lay the strips over the beans. Cover the pot and bake for 4 hours or until tender. Periodically check the beans to see that they are covered with liquid; if necessary, add boiling water to keep them covered. The liquid will thicken as it cooks. Remove the pot from the oven and stir in the ketchup and vinegar. Taste and adjust the seasoning, if necessary. Serve hot.

Chef's Tip: Use dry sun-dried tomatoes, not the ones packed in oil, for this recipe. The tomatoes will plump up as they cook.

COLE SLAW
Serves 8 as a side dish

⅔ cup sour cream
⅔ cup mayonnaise
¼ cup apple cider vinegar
2 teaspoons mustard
2 teaspoons sugar
1 teaspoon celery seed
Salt and freshly ground pepper to taste
1 head green cabbage, thinly sliced (about 6 cups)
1 red onion, thinly sliced
1 carrot, grated

Combine the sour cream, mayonnaise, vinegar, mustard, sugar, and celery seed in a large bowl. Add the salt and pepper. Add the remaining ingredients and stir until the slaw is evenly coated. Taste and adjust the seasoning, if necessary. Cover and refrigerate 1 to 2 hours before serving.

PASTA SALAD
Serves 8 as a side dish

8 ounces rotelle or penne pasta
2 tablespoons white balsamic vinegar (see Chef's Tip)
1 garlic clove, minced
Salt and cracked pepper to taste
¼ cup olive oil
1 head broccoli, cut into florets
  (about 2 cups) and blanched (page 103)
¾ cup (6-ounces) marinated artichoke hearts
½ cup small dice mixed red and green pepper
⅓ cup black and or green olives, pitted and halved
2 tablespoons grated Parmesan, plus more if needed
12 basil leaves, chopped

(continued on next page)

Cook the pasta in a large pot of salted boiling water for 12 to 15 minutes, or until al dente. Drain well and let cool to room temperature.

Combine the vinegar, garlic, salt, and pepper in a large bowl. Gradually whisk in the oil until thoroughly combined. Add the pasta, broccoli, and remaining ingredients. Toss to coat the pasta evenly. Add salt, pepper, and additional Parmesan to taste. Serve at room temperature or chilled.

Chef's Tip: If white balsamic vinegar (also known as "sweet wine vinegar") is not available, use white wine vinegar plus ½ teaspoon sugar.

SPRING CHICKEN AND MORE

Certified Master Chef Tim Ryan

Spring Chicken and More is a special menu for two. Prepare and enjoy this menu with a good friend to celebrate spring as it turns to summer and the first fruits of the earth are ready to harvest. Like all the great classic dishes, these simple seasonal recipes are best made with herbs and vegetables picked right from the garden. At our Greystone campus in St. Helena, California, our students and chefs can do just that, as the Canard Herb Garden and the Sutter Home Organic Garden are just footsteps from the teaching kitchens and restaurant.

SALMON SCALLOPS WITH SORREL SAUCE
Serves 2 as a first course

SAUCE BASE

1 cup Fish Broth (page 107) or Chicken Broth
   (page 107)
2 tablespoons dry white wine
1 tablespoon arrowroot or cornstarch
1 tablespoon cold water
¼ cup evaporated skim milk
Salt and freshly ground pepper to taste

One 6-ounce salmon fillet
Salt and freshly ground pepper to taste
1 tablespoon vegetable oil
2 cups tightly packed sorrel leaves, cut into shreds
1 tablespoon fresh lemon juice, plus more if needed
1 tablespoon unsalted butter (optional)

To make the sauce base: Combine the broth and wine in a medium saucepan and bring to a boil over high heat. Combine the arrowroot or cornstarch and water in a cup and whisk to blend. Add this mixture to the broth mixture in the pan and return it to a boil. Add the evaporated skim milk and bring the sauce base to a boil, stirring constantly. Season with salt and pepper. Strain the sauce base through a fine-meshed sieve and set aside.

Cut the salmon horizontally into 2 thin slices. Place the slices between 2 pieces of waxed paper or plastic wrap and flatten them lightly with the smooth side of a mallet or the bottom of a heavy pan. Season the salmon with salt and pepper. Heat the oil in a large nonstick or seasoned cast-iron skillet until it is almost smoking. Cook the salmon for 1 minute on the first side. Turn over and cook for 1 minute on the second side. Remove the salmon from the skillet and pat the excess oil from it with paper towels.

(continued on next page)

To finish the sauce: Return the sauce base to a boil and stir in the shredded sorrel and lemon juice. Swirl in the butter, if desired, until it is just melted and blended into the sauce. Taste and adjust the seasoning with lemon juice, salt, and pepper, if necessary.

To serve, ladle the sorrel sauce onto warmed plates, place the salmon on top of the sauce, and serve at once.

POACHED SPRING CHICKEN WITH GARDEN VEGETABLES AND TARRAGON
Serves 2 as a main course

One 2¼ pound broiler chicken or Cornish game hen
Salt and freshly ground pepper to taste
2 thyme sprigs
1 bay leaf
4 flat-leaf parsley sprigs
8 cups Chicken Broth, or as needed (page 107)
6 whole baby carrots, peeled
4 whole baby turnips, peeled
2 ounces haricots verts, ends trimmed
   (see Chef's Tips)
1 cup cooked brown rice (page 106)
2 tablespoons chopped fresh tarragon
1 tablespoon chopped fresh chervil or parsley

Remove any excess fat from the cavity of the chicken. Rinse the chicken under cold running water and pat dry with paper towels. Season the chicken, including the cavity, with salt and pepper. Put the thyme, bay leaf, and parsley in the body cavity of the chicken. Truss the chicken with butcher's twine (page 104).

Bring 4 cups of the chicken broth to a boil in a medium saucepan. Add the carrots and cook until they are tender, about 8 to 10 minutes. Using a slotted spoon, transfer the carrots to a bowl of cold water to stop the cooking process. Once cooled, remove the carrots from the water, drain, and set aside. Repeat this process, to cook the turnips (6 to 8 minutes) and haricots verts (3 to 4 minutes) separately in the same broth, then cooling and draining them. Reserve the broth and vegetables separately until needed.

Place the chicken in a pot large enough to hold it while leaving about ½ inch of space around the chicken. Pour all of the broth (including that used to cook the vegetables) over the chicken. It should cover the chicken by ½ inch. If you don't have quite enough broth, add water. Bring the broth to a simmer over medium heat. Reduce heat to low and simmer gently for about 1 hour, or until the chicken is tender and the juices run clear when a thigh is pierced.

Remove the chicken from the pot. Add the vegetables, rice, and herbs to the broth. While the vegetables and rice are reheating, carve the chicken into serving pieces. Season the broth to taste with salt and pepper. Place the chicken meat into warmed soup plates. Spoon the broth over the chicken and scatter the vegetables and rice around the pieces.

Chef's Tips: Haricots verts are very slender green beans. They are frequently available in the spring or early summer. If they are unavailable, use the thinnest green beans you can find.

Other vegetables such as fava beans, summer squash, mushrooms, peas, parsnips, and so on, can be added as available and desired.

GLAZED PINEAPPLE WITH GREEN PEPPERCORNS AND RICOTTA "ICE CREAM"
Serves 2

RICOTTA "ICE CREAM"
  1 cup part-skim ricotta cheese
  ¾ cup nonfat plain yogurt
  ½ cup maple syrup
  1½ teaspoons vanilla extract

GLAZED PINEAPPLE
  ¼ teaspoon green peppercorns,
     drained, rinsed, and mashed
  2 cored fresh pineapple slices, ½ inch thick
  2 tablespoons sugar
  ¼ cup fresh orange juice
  1½ teaspoons honey
  1 tablespoon light rum

To make the "ice cream": Purée the ricotta cheese in a food processor until very smooth. Add the yogurt, maple syrup, and vanilla, and purée until smooth. Transfer the mixture to an ice cream machine and freeze according to the manufacturer's instructions. Transfer the frozen "ice cream" to a clean container, cover tightly and place in freezer until needed. (See Chef's Tip.)

To prepare the glazed pineapple: Rub the peppercorns evenly over the surface of the pineapple, then sprinkle one side of each slice evenly with sugar. Combine the orange juice, honey, and rum in a small bowl.

Heat a medium sauté pan over high heat until it is smoking hot. Place the pineapple slices in the pan, sugared-side down. Cook until the sugar is browned and there is a distinct caramel smell, about 1 to 2 minutes. Turn the pineapple and cook the second side until browned, about 1 minute. Transfer the pineapple to a plate. Add the juice mixture to the pan and cook over high heat until it has reduced to the consistency of maple syrup. Pour this sauce over the pineapple, top with a scoop of the ricotta "ice cream," and serve at once.

Chef's Tip: The ricotta "ice cream" will keep in the freezer for up to 3 days; after that it tends to become icy. If you prefer, substitute frozen vanilla yogurt or ice cream.

SCRUMPTIOUS SUMMER DESSERTS

Certified Master Pastry Chef Markus Färbinger

The scrumptious summer desserts I offer you are elegant and traditional yet easy to prepare. Apricot-Chocolate Marrakech is a tasty tart made with dark chocolate and fresh apricots from Morocco. I prefer to use raspberries or blackberries in my Berry Napoleon, but almost any fruit may be used.

Both desserts share a secret recipe, express puff pastry, that was passed down to me from my father. It is an excellent substitute for traditional puff pastry, which is time-consuming and laborious to make. One day during my father's apprenticeship in Switzerland, he arrived at the bakery too late to make the puff pastry dough. He decided to use the express puff pastry method and discovered that his boss was none the wiser. Ever since then, he has used the express method, saving himself a lot of time. I could not believe my father strayed from tradition! But years later, we compared the two methods side by side and now I, too, use the express method exclusively.

EXPRESS PUFF PASTRY
Makes 3 pounds dough

1¼ pounds all-purpose or cake flour
1 cup plus 6 tablespoons ice water
1 tablespoon salt
1 pound (4 sticks) unsalted butter, cut into large dice

Combine all the ingredients in a food processor. Pulse until barely mixed. To mix by hand, combine the flour and butter pieces in a large bowl. Toss until all the butter is coated with flour. Add the water and salt and mix until a shaggy mass is formed. Turn the mixture out onto a lightly floured marble slab or other cool surface. Shape the mixture into a square. Roll the dough into a rectangular piece, ½ inch thick. Fold the right and left edges of the dough into the center of the rectangle so they meet and do not overlap. Fold the dough in half at the center seam to create 4 layers.

Repeat the roll-and-fold procedure. Tightly cover the 4 layer rectangle in plastic wrap and refrigerate for at least 2 and up to 24 hours. The dough should be firm, yet pliable, before you do the final roll-and-fold.

Repeat the roll-and-fold process two more times for a total of 4 folds. The dough is now ready to roll, cut, and shape as desired.

Chef's Tip: Once the dough has been properly rolled and folded, it may be tightly wrapped in plastic wrap and stored in the refrigerator for up to 3 days or in the freezer for up to 4 weeks.

APRICOT-CHOCOLATE MARRAKECH
Serves 8

PASTRY SHELL
1 pound Express Puff Pastry (page 56)
1 egg, beaten
4 ounces semisweet chocolate, melted

FILLING
¾ cup heavy cream
8 ounces semisweet chocolate, chopped
2 tablespoons honey
4 tablespoons (½ stick) unsalted butter
    at room temperature
2 tablespoons Frangelico or dark rum
16 pieces Poached Apricots in Lemon-Vanilla Syrup,
    drained (page 89)

GARNISH
Powdered sugar for dusting
Chocolate curls

To make the shell: Preheat the oven to 375°F. On a lightly floured surface, roll the puff pastry into a 12-by-5 inch strip that is ⅛-inch thick. Cut off two ½-by-12 inch strips. Prick the surface of the large rectangle. Brush the edges with the beaten egg. Lay the ½-inch strips along both long sides of the large rectangle to create a border. Using a sharp knife, cut small incisions in the strips, ½ inch apart. Brush the beaten egg on the strips. Place the shell on a baking sheet and bake for 12 to 15 minutes, or until golden brown. Let cool to room temperature. Brush the bottom of the cooled pastry shell with the melted chocolate.

To make the filling: Bring the heavy cream to a boil in a saucepan over medium heat. Put the chocolate in a large bowl and pour the hot cream and the honey over the chocolate. Using a whisk, stir the filling until it is thoroughly combined. Add the butter and Frangelico or rum and stir gently until incorporated. Set aside let cool to room temperature.

To assemble: Place the drained apricot pieces in the bottom of the tart shell. Spread the chocolate cream evenly over the apricots. Refrigerate, uncovered, for about 2 hours, or until set.

To serve, dust lightly with powdered sugar and cut into 8 slices. Garnish each slice with chocolate curls.

BERRY NAPOLEON
Serves 8

12 ounces Express Puff Pastry (page 56)
Powdered sugar for dusting

CRÈME LÉGER
1 cup milk
⅓ cup plus 2 tablespoons granulated sugar
2 tablespoons cornstarch
2 tablespoons all-purpose flour
3 egg yolks
1 teaspoon vanilla extract
1 tablespoon dark rum
2 cups heavy cream

4 pints fresh raspberries
8 lemon balm sprigs or mint leaves

Preheat the oven to 375°F. Line a baking pan with parchment paper. On a lightly floured surface, roll the puff pastry out into a 12-by-16-inch rectangle about ⅛ inch thick. Using the tines of a fork, prick the pastry all over. Place the pastry on the prepared pan. Cover the pastry with a second piece of parchment paper and top with another baking sheet. Bake the pastry for 15 minutes. Remove the top baking sheet and parchment paper and generously dust the pastry with powdered sugar. Increase the oven temperature to 425°F. Bake the pastry 5 minutes longer, or until the sugar turns a dark golden brown. Remove the pastry from the oven and let cool completely in the pan.

To make the crème léger: Bring the milk just to a boil in a small saucepan. Set aside. Blend ⅓ cup granulated sugar, cornstarch, and flour in another small saucepan. Add the yolks and stir. Add the hot milk in a stream, whisking constantly. Cook over medium heat, stirring constantly with a whisk, until the mixture comes to a boil. Simmer for 3 minutes over low heat, stirring constantly. Strain the mixture into a large bowl. Stir in the vanilla and rum. Set aside and let cool.

Using an electric mixer or a whisk, beat the cream and remaining 2 tablespoons sugar in a large, chilled bowl until medium-stiff peaks form. Gently fold the whipped cream into the cooled mixture. Place the crème léger in a pastry bag fitted with a large tip and set aside.

Cut the pastry into twenty-four 2-by-4-inch rectangles. Reserve 8 of the best looking rectangles for the napoleon tops. Lay out 8 rectangles. Cover each rectangle with berries and pipe the crème léger over the berries. Top each napoleon with a second layer of pastry and make another layer of berries and crème léger. Top each napoleon with one of the rectangles reserved for the tops. Dust with powdered sugar and garnish with raspberries and lemon balm or mint.

MEDITERRANEAN MAGIC FOR FATHER'S DAY

Chef Paul Sartory

As a child, I loved to fish with my father. As a dad, I love to fish with my kids. This simple fish dish was inspired by my childhood memories of returning from an early-morning fishing trip with my dad, cleaning our catch, and immediately grilling it in the backyard.

As chef at the Wine Spectator Greystone Restaurant, I still employ this simple, direct style of cooking. The Mediterranean menu reflects our commitment to buy fresh, local products and prepare them in a manner that highlights their natural flavors. Most dishes are served in their own juices without any distracting sauces.

GRILLED FISH WITH THYME
Serves 6 as a first course

6 sea bream, pan-ready (see Chef's Tips)
Juice of ½ lemon
Salt and freshly ground pepper to taste
1½ tablespoons olive oil
12 thyme sprigs
1½ pounds asparagus, trimmed and blanched
   (page 103), see Chef's Tips
6 lemon wedges for garnish

Preheat a grill to medium heat. Clean the cooking rack thoroughly and brush it with oil.

Rinse the fish thoroughly under cold running water and pat it dry with paper towels. Drizzle the cavity of each fish with the lemon juice, a pinch of salt and pepper, and a little oil. Place 2 thyme sprigs in each fish.

Grill the fish over medium heat for about 3 minutes on the first side, or until the skin of the fish has blistered and is marked. Carefully turn the fish and grill for 3 minutes on the second side. Grill the asparagus for a total of 1 to 2 minutes, turning occasionally to cook evenly.

To serve, place the fish and asparagus on a warmed serving platter or individual plates. Sprinkle with salt and pepper and garnish with lemon wedges.

Chef's Tips: Sea bream is a small fish suitable for a single portion. If sea bream is not available in your area, try trout, coho salmon, mackerel, or other single-portion-sized fish. Pan-ready fish should be scaled and gutted (drawn). The head, fins, and tail may be removed or not, according to the type of fish and your personal preference. The fishmonger can do this for you.

If the asparagus are no thicker than a pencil, they need not be blanched before grilling.

ROSEMARY-SKEWERED CHICKEN AND MUSHROOM KABOBS
Serves 6 as a main course

MARINADE
  ½ cup olive oil
  3 tablespoons fresh lemon juice
  1 tablespoon dried Mediterranean oregano
  1 teaspoon minced garlic
  ½ teaspoon salt
  ½ teaspoon ground pepper

  12 skinless, boneless chicken thighs
  30 medium mushrooms
  6 rosemary skewers (see Chef's Tips)
  Grilled Flatbread (recipe follows)

To make the marinade: Combine all the marinade ingredients in a medium bowl and whisk until blended.

Trim any fat from each thigh. Cut the thighs in half and transfer to a large bowl. Pour two thirds of the marinade over the thighs, and turn them until they are coated evenly.

Add the mushrooms to the remaining marinade and toss to coat evenly. Let the chicken and mushrooms marinate at room temperature for 30 minutes.

Preheat a grill to medium heat. Assemble the kabobs by alternately threading 6 mushrooms and 3 pieces of chicken on each rosemary branch, beginning and ending with 2 mushrooms. Grill the kabobs, turning to cook evenly, for a total of 15 to 20 minutes, or until the chicken is browned on the outside and opaque in the interior.

During the last 2 to 3 minutes of cooking time, place the flatbread on the grill to reheat, turning once.

To serve, place a skewer in the center of a piece of grilled flatbread, fold the bread around the meat, and pull the skewer out, leaving the chicken and mushrooms inside the bread. Serve a second piece of grilled bread along with the meal.

Chef's Tip: Long rosemary stems (about 8 to 10 inches long) may often be found in the produce section of supermarkets or specialty foods stores. Strip the leaves from all but the last inch of the stem. Reserve the leaves for other recipes.

GRILLED FLATBREAD
Serves 6; makes 12 flatbreads

  1½ packages active dry yeast
  2 cups warm (105° to 115°F) water
  1 tablespoon sugar
  4 tablespoons olive oil, plus more as needed for brushing
  2 cups semolina flour
  3 cups bread flour, or as needed
  2 teaspoons kosher salt

Combine the yeast and warm water in a large bowl and let sit for 10 minutes, or until a thick foam develops. Stir in the sugar and 2 tablespoons of the oil. Whisk the semolina flour, ½ cup at a time, into the yeast mixture. Gradually blend in 1 cup of the bread flour. Stir well with a wooden spoon for about 5 minutes. Continue to add the remaining flour, a ½ cup at a time, until a smooth, heavy dough forms. Turn the dough out onto a lightly floured work surface. Knead for about 5 minutes, or until the dough is very smooth, elastic, and springy. Add more flour as you knead to prevent sticking, if necessary.

Lightly oil a large bowl, add the dough, and turn until it is coated. Cover the bowl with a clean towel and let the dough rise in a warm place until doubled, about 1 to 1½ hours. Punch the dough down and divide it into 12 equal balls. Roll and stretch each ball on a lightly floured work surface into a circle about ¼ inch thick. Place the shaped dough on baking sheets that have been sprinkled with cornmeal. Cover the flatbread pieces and let them rise for 30 minutes.

Preheat a grill to medium-low heat. Brush the dough lightly with the remaining 2 tablespoons olive oil. Place the flatbread on the grill, cover, and cook for 1 to 2 minutes on one side, or until bubbles appear on the top. Turn, cover, and cook for 1 to 2 minutes on the second side, or until the bread is light brown on both sides but still pliable. (This may be done in batches if necessary.) Stack the cooked flatbreads in a napkin-lined basket to keep them warm. Serve warm.

Chef's Tip: This recipe will make enough flatbread to serve 1 piece with each skewer. Serve the others on the side to mop up the juices.

LAVENDER FLANS
Makes 6 individual flans

CUSTARD
  2 cups milk
  ½ cup sugar
  1 tablespoon chopped fresh lavender,
    or 1½ teaspoons dried lavender, crumbled
  3 eggs
  2 egg yolks

CARAMEL
  ⅔ cup sugar
  3 to 4 drops fresh lemon juice
  2 tablespoons water

GARNISH
  1 pint fresh strawberries, hulled and quartered
  6 fresh mint leaves

To make the custard: Combine the milk, ¼ cup of the sugar, and the lavender in a medium saucepan and bring to a boil over medium-high heat. Remove from heat and let sit for at least 30 minutes.

Combine the eggs, egg yolks, and remaining ¼ cup sugar in a medium bowl and beat until light and frothy. Gradually add half the boiled milk mixture, stirring constantly. Gradually add the yolk mixture back to the milk mixture in the pan, stirring constantly. Strain the custard into a clean container and let cool to room temperature. Cover and refrigerate overnight. (This may be done 1 day in advance.)

To make the caramel: Lightly oil six 4-ounce ramekins or custard cups. Combine all the caramel ingredients in a small saucepan. Cook over medium heat, stirring occasionally, until the sugar turns a light amber color, about 10 to 12 minutes. Pour an ⅛-inch layer of caramel into the bottom of each prepared ramekin or custard cup.

To make the flans: Preheat the oven to 325°F. Place the ramekins or cups in a deep baking pan. Carefully pour the custard into the ramekins or cups. Add warm water halfway up the sides of the ramekins or cups. Bake for 25 to 30 minutes, or until the edges have set and a nickel-sized spot in the center jiggles slightly when a flan is shaken. Remove the baking pan from the oven and remove the flans from the baking pan. Let cool completely.

Tip each flan out of the ramekin or cup onto a dessert plate and garnish with strawberries and mint.

SUMMER SIZZLE ON THE GRILL

Chef Bob Briggs

In the middle of summer, who wants to cook inside? My Summer Sizzle on the Grill menu offers chicken and bread recipes you would normally expect to prepare in an oven. The chicken is marinated in garlic and lime, an excellent combination. The marinade is also used to baste the chicken as it rotates on the spit. The bread, an olive and rosemary focaccia, takes on a hint of smoke from the grill. Penne pasta with pesto is a great way to showcase the first basil from my garden. A Chianti granita with summer berries is a cool and refreshing way to end the meal. Try other wine and berry combinations to suit your personal taste.

BLACK OLIVE AND ROSEMARY FOCACCIA
Serves 8; makes two 8-inch round breads

¾ cup lukewarm (105° to 115°F) water
2¾ cups bread flour, plus more as needed
1 package active dry yeast
¼ teaspoon sugar or honey
½ teaspoon salt

24 black olives, preferably Calamata,
    pitted and halved
1 teaspoon chopped fresh rosemary
Freshly cracked pepper to taste
Extra-virgin olive oil for brushing
Salt to taste

Combine the water, 1¾ cups of the flour, the yeast, and sugar or honey in a large bowl, or the bowl of heavy-duty mixer fitted with a dough hook to make the "sponge." Whisk or mix until thoroughly combined. Cover and let sit in a warm place for 45 minutes to 1 hour. The sponge should be thick, foamy, and bubbly with a strong yeasty aroma.

Add the remaining 1 cup flour and the salt to the sponge and mix to blend. Knead the dough by hand on a lightly floured board or knead the dough with the dough hook for 10 minutes, or until a smooth, elastic dough is formed. Add a little flour as needed to keep the dough from sticking.

Shape the dough into a ball and rub it lightly with olive oil. Place it in a large bowl, cover with a damp towel or plastic wrap, and let the dough rise in a warm place for 1 to 2 hours, or until doubled in size.

Punch down the dough and divide it into 2 equal pieces. Shape the dough into rounds and let them rest while preparing the pans. Lightly coat two 8-inch round cake pans with olive oil and sprinkle them generously with cornmeal. Gently tap out the excess.

Place a ball of dough in the center of each pan. With your fingertips, push the dough out, working from the center, until it covers the pan. (If the dough sticks to your fingers, dip them in some olive oil.) Place half of the olives on each round and press them into the dough. Sprinkle with the rosemary and pepper. Shape the remaining dough and top in the same way. Cover the pans with a damp towel and let rise in a warm place until nearly doubled in size, about 45 minutes.

Preheat a grill to high heat. Place the pans on the upper shelf of the grill and cover the grill. Cook the focaccia for 15 to 20 minutes, or until the edges are brown and slightly pulled away from the sides and the bottom is crisp. Transfer the focaccia from the pans to wire racks and, while still warm, drizzle or brush generously with extra-virgin olive oil and sprinkle with salt.

Cut into wedges and serve warm or at room temperature.

Chef's Tip: The focaccia can also be baked in a preheated 475°F oven.

SPIT-ROASTED GARLIC AND LIME CHICKEN
Serves 4 as a main course

One 3- to 3½-pound chicken
5 limes, juiced and 4 rind halves reserved
2 tablespoons coarsely chopped garlic
1 teaspoon Asian sesame oil
1 teaspoon salt
½ teaspoon cracked pepper
½ cup Chicken Broth (page 107), plus more if needed

Rinse the chicken under cold running water and pat dry with paper towels. Fill the cavity of the chicken with the lime rinds. Truss the chicken with butcher's twine (page 104) and place it in a heavy self-sealing plastic bag. Combine the lime juice, garlic, sesame oil, salt, and pepper in a small bowl to make a marinade. Pour the marinade into the bag with the chicken and seal tightly. Let the chicken marinate for 2 hours in the refrigerator, turning it occasionally. Remove the chicken from the bag, reserving the marinade.

Preheat a grill with an electric rotisserie to high heat. (To cook directly on a grill, see Chef's Tips.) Place the chicken on the rotisserie and lower the heat to medium. Pour the chicken broth into a shallow pan and place it under the chicken to collect the drippings. Close the cover on the grill and spit-roast the chicken for 1 hour, or until an instant-read thermometer inserted in a thigh registers 165°F. Periodically baste the chicken with the reserved marinade. When all of the marinade has been used, continue to baste with the drippings that have collected in the pan with the chicken broth. If necessary, add more chicken broth or water to the pan so the drippings do not burn. Remove the chicken from the rotisserie and let sit for 20 minutes before carving.

Chef's Tips: This recipe may be easily doubled to serve 8.
To grill the chicken instead of spit-roasting, halved or quarter the chicken. Preheat the grill to medium heat. Grill the chicken for 10 minutes, turning occasionally, until evenly seared. Cover the grill and continue to cook for another 45 to 50 minutes, or until the juices from the thickest piece of the chicken run clear. Baste the chicken and turn it from time to time so that it cooks evenly.

GRILLED SUMMER VEGETABLES WITH BALSAMIC VINAIGRETTE
Serves 8 as a side dish

2 *each* red and green peppers, seeded, deribbed,
   and cut into 4-inch wide strips
2 yellow squash, cut lengthwise
   into ¼-inch-thick slices
2 zucchini, cut lengthwise into ¼-inch-thick slices
2 Japanese eggplants, cut lengthwise
   into ¼-inch-thick slices
Balsamic Vinaigrette (recipe follows)
Shaved Parmesan (page 104),
   or ½ cup grated Parmesan

(continued on next page)

Preheat a grill to high heat. Combine the vegetables and vinaigrette in a large bowl and toss. Drain the vegetables, reserving the vinaigrette.

Grill the peppers, skin-side down, until the skin blisters and chars. Remove the peppers and scrape off the charred skin. Grill the yellow squash, zucchini, and eggplant for about 2 minutes on each side, or until they are tender. Place all the grilled vegetables on a platter or in a bowl and drizzle with the reserved vinaigrette. Top with shaved or grated Parmesan. Serve at once.

BALSAMIC VINAIGRETTE
Makes ¾ cup

½ cup balsamic vinegar
2 teaspoons chopped fresh oregano
½ teaspoon salt, or to taste
½ teaspoon cracked black pepper
¼ cup extra-virgin olive oil

Combine the vinegar, oregano, salt, and pepper in a small bowl. Gradually whisk in the oil until thoroughly blended.

Chef's Tip: Whisk this vinaigrette to recombine it just before you add it to the grilled vegetables.

TOMATO, ARUGULA, AND MOZZARELLA SALAD
Serve 8 as a salad course

6 ripe tomatoes, cut into ¼-inch-thick slices
12 ounces fresh mozzarella,
    cut into ¼-inch-thick slices
½ cup extra-virgin olive oil
¼ cup red wine vinegar
2 bunches arugula, stemmed
Kosher salt and freshly cracked pepper to taste
12 basil leaves, thinly sliced, for garnish

Overlap alternating tomato and mozzarella slices around the edge of a platter. Whisk the olive oil and vinegar together in a small bowl. Combine the arugula with half of the oil-and-vinegar mixture in a large bowl and toss. Place the arugula in the center of the platter. Drizzle the remaining oil-and-vinegar mixture over the tomatoes and mozzarella. Sprinkle with the salt and pepper and garnish with basil.

CHIANTI GRANITA WITH SUMMER BERRIES
Serves 8

¾ cup warm water
1 cup sugar
1½ cups Chianti wine
⅓ cup fresh lemon juice
⅓ cup fresh orange juice
2 cups fresh raspberries, blueberries, blackberries,
    red currants, and/or sliced strawberries
12 mint leaves, thinly sliced, for garnish

Chill 8 serving bowls or wineglasses in the freezer.

Combine the warm water and sugar in a large bowl. Add the wine, lemon, and orange juice. Pour the mixture into an 9-by-13-inch metal pan and place it in the freezer. Periodically stir the mixture until it is completely frozen, about 4 to 5 hours. The granita will have a very granular consistency. With a sturdy spoon or ice cream scoop, scrape out the granita into the chilled serving bowls or wineglasses. Top with fresh berries and garnish with the sliced mint leaves.

Grilled Summer Vegetables with Balsamic Vinaigrette
Page 63

Fusion Gazpacho: A Salad, Salsa, or Soup
Page 88

Marinated Grilled Lamb Chops and Summer Stew Au Pistou
Page 93

Grilled Fish with Thyme
Page 59

Barbecued Spareribs with Pasta Salad and Corn Bread with Cheddar Cheese and Roasted Corn
Pages 49, 50 and 51

Braised Chicken with Lemon Zest, Olives, and Creamy Polenta
Page 21

Capellini with Grilled Vegetable Ragout
Page 91

Salmon-Wrapped Asparagus with Chive Sauce
Page 24

AN ALL-AMERICAN FOURTH OF JULY MEAL

Certified Master Chef Tim Ryan

This All-American Fourth of July menu of Caesar's salad, shore dinner, and yogurt and berry cream parfait offers exciting recipes to prepare for the country's most exciting day of the year.

Despite its Roman sounding name, Caesar salad was invented in Mexico and has become a favorite on restaurant menus throughout the United States. A great Caesar salad is easy to make at home.

For me, the Fourth of July conjures up the images of barbecues in the backyard and clambakes down by the seashore. A traditional clambake can be a bit complicated and the timing can be tricky. The following recipe does not require a beach, nor is it difficult to do. I prefer the term shore dinner to clambake, to emphasize the variety of shellfish and fish in this meal.

The red, white, and blue colors of the dessert make it a perfect choice for the Fourth of July.

CAESAR SALAD
Serves 4

DRESSING
1 egg yolk (see Chef's Tips)
2 tablespoons fresh lemon juice
1 tablespoon Dijon mustard
3 whole anchovies (optional)
2 garlic cloves, minced
1 cup olive oil
¼ cup grated Parmesan
6 tablespoons water
1 tablespoon chopped fresh flat-leaf parsley
Salt and finely ground pepper to taste

Hearts from 2 heads romaine lettuce,
    torn into bite-sized pieces
1 cup plain croutons (page 104)

To make the dressing: Combine the egg yolk, lemon juice, mustard, anchovies, and garlic in a blender or food processor and process until smooth. With the machine still running, gradually pour in the olive oil. Add the cheese and water. Process until the dressing is totally homogenous. Add the parsley, salt, and pepper.

Put the lettuce in a large bowl. Add the dressing and toss to coat the lettuce evenly. (Be careful not to overdress the salad.) Add the croutons, toss, and serve on chilled plates.

Chef's Tips: The egg yolk in this dressing may be replaced with a pasteurized egg yolk, available in the dairy or frozen food case in most grocery stores.

Any unused dressing may be covered and stored in the refrigerator for up to 24 hours.

SURE-FIRE SHORE DINNER
Serves 4

2 tablespoons unsalted butter
1 cup finely chopped onions
1 teaspoon minced garlic
2 cups Chicken Broth (page 107)
1 cup water
2 thyme sprigs
2 small bay leaves
2 handfuls fresh seaweed
Two 1¼-pound live lobsters
16 littleneck clams, scrubbed
2 small zucchini, halved lengthwise
    and cut into quarters
12 Red Bliss potatoes, cooked (page 103)
4 small chicken thighs (optional; see Chef's Tip)
One 8-ounce cod fillet
4 ears corn on the cob, shucked and halved crosswise
20 mussels, scrubbed and debearded
2 leeks, white part only, split lengthwise
    and blanched (page 103)
8 sea scallops (optional)
¼ cup chopped fresh flat-leaf parsley
Lemon wedges for garnish
¾ cup clarified butter (page 104)

You will need a large steamer with a two-tiered steaming basket. Melt the butter in the bottom of the steamer over medium heat. Add the onions and garlic and cook until their aromas are released. Add the broth, water, thyme sprig, and bay leaves and bring to a boil.

Make a bed of seaweed on the bottom of the steaming basket. Kill the lobsters by making a small incision in the back of the shell where the chest and tail meet. Place the lobsters on top of the seaweed and top them with the clams, zucchini, potatoes, and optional chicken thighs. Place the basket over the boiling broth. Cover the steamer and cook for 5 to 8 minutes.

While the first tier is cooking, arrange the cod, corn, mussels, leeks and optional scallops on the steamer's second tier. Add the second tier to the steamer, cover, and continue to steam for another 5 minutes, or until the clams and mussels are open; the lobsters, cod, and optional scallops and chicken are opaque throughout; and the vegetables are tender.

Remove the lobsters from the steamer and split in half. Remove all the other food and arrange it in warmed casseroles or serving bowls. Sprinkle with chopped parsley and moisten with the broth. Serve with lemon wedges and clarified butter.

Chef's Tip: To cook this dish on the grill, bring the broth to a boil by placing it directly over the heating elements or the hottest coals. Proceed as directed in the recipe; the cooking time will remain the same. You may wish to precook the chicken thighs by grilling, poaching, or baking in order to be sure they are fully cooked. Precooking time for average-sized thighs is 10 minutes on a hot grill, 15 minutes in simmering broth, or 20 minutes in a 350°F oven.

YOGURT CREAM AND BERRY PARFAIT
Serves 4

FRUIT LAYER

1 pint fresh strawberries, hulled
1 cup fresh blueberries
1 cup fresh raspberries
¼ cup sugar
1 tablespoon kirschwasser

YOGURT CREAM

½ cup heavy cream
1 cup plain yogurt
1 tablespoon sugar
¼ teaspoon fresh lemon juice
1 tablespoon kirschwasser (optional)
1½ teaspoons plain gelatin
1 tablespoon water

CHERRY LAYER

½ cup cherry juice (See Chef's Tip)
1 tablespoon sugar
¼ teaspoon fresh lemon juice
½ teaspoon cornstarch
1 tablespoon water
1 tablespoon kirschwasser

Sweetened whipped cream for garnish (optional)

To make the fruit layer: Cut the strawberries in halves or quarters, depending on their size. Combine ½ cup strawberries and ½ cup raspberries in a blender and purée. Add the sugar and kirschwasser and purée. Strain through a fine-meshed sieve.

Spoon 2 tablespoons of the berry purée into each of 4 parfait glasses. Place one fourth of the remaining strawberries in each glass, then top with a layer of one fourth of the blueberries and a layer of one fourth of the raspberries, filling each glass almost three-fourths full. Pour the remaining berry purée on top.

To make the yogurt cream: Whip the cream in a deep bowl until soft peaks form. Add the yogurt, sugar, lemon juice, and kirschwasser and whip until smooth. Do not over whip.

In a small bowl, combine the gelatin and water. Let sit for 5 minutes, then heat over barely simmering water, stirring constantly, until the gelatin is dissolved. Whisk the gelatin mixture into the yogurt mixture. Divide among the parfait glasses, leaving ½ inch of space at the top of each glass. Refrigerate for at least 1 hour.

To make the cherry layer: Combine the cherry juice, sugar, and lemon juice in a small saucepan and bring to a boil. Combine the cornstarch and the water in a cup and whisk into cherry juice mixture. Add the kirschwasser, set aside, and let cool. Pour the cherry layer on top of yogurt cream. Refrigerate the parfaits for 30 minutes before serving. Garnish with sweetened whipped cream, if desired.

Chef's Tip: Cherry juice may be purchased in natural foods stores or made from fresh cherries using an electric juicer.

SEASONAL SALADS

Chef Catherine Brandel

Much of my cooking is inspired by the time I spent in the kitchen at Chez Panisse. The tuna confit, for example, is a method I learned from a wonderfully energetic and innovative cook from London who spent six months working there. The success of the shaved vegetable salad depends on something else that was always stressed: Everything must be impeccably fresh and you must taste it before you decide to include it. For example, if the squash makes your mouth pucker or the radishes are bitter, leave them out and just add a little more of something else. Use your imagination.

TUNA CONFIT WITH MEYER LEMON SALSA AND SHAVED VEGETABLE SALAD

Serves 6 as a salad course; makes about 2 cups tuna confit

1 pound tuna, cut into 1-inch-thick slices (see Chef's Tips)
3½ teaspoons kosher salt
8 fennel sprigs
6 basil stems
6 thyme stems
4 bay leaves
4 garlic cloves, quartered
2 jalapeño chilies, halved lengthwise
3½ cups olive oil (see Chef's Tips)
Meyer Lemon Salsa (recipe follows)
Shaved Vegetable Salad (recipe follows)

Sprinkle the tuna evenly on all sides with the salt and place it in a pan large enough to hold the tuna in a single layer. Cover the pan and refrigerate overnight.

Put the fennel, basil, thyme, and bay leaves on a work surface and gently bruise them with the back of a wooden spoon, or lightly crush them in your hands. Combine the bruised herbs, garlic, jalapeños, and olive oil in a large saucepan. Bring the oil to a bare simmer (160°F) over low heat, and cook for about 20 minutes. The garlic should not brown.

To make the confit: Using a slotted spatula, remove the tuna from the pan, allowing any juices drawn from the fish to drain away. Add the tuna to the hot oil and cook over very low heat, for 5 to 8 minutes, or until barely pink in the center. Transfer the fish to a clean bowl. Strain the oil and let cool. Pour the cooled oil over the fish and let sit for 3 hours at room temperature. (The tuna may be refrigerated now, if you will be serving it later.)

Using a slotted spoon, remove the tuna from the oil and flake it apart or break it into chunks. Serve the confit with the salad on a chilled platter or individual serving plates. Top with a spoonful of salsa and serve with shaved vegetable salad.

Chef's Tips: Good-sized tuna "trimmings" may also be used. If the pieces are smaller than 1 inch, use less salt and just enough oil to cover the fish.

The tuna in oil will keep in the refrigerator for 3 days. Let it come to room temperature before draining, flaking, and serving.

Tuna confit can be used for salad niçoise or other recipes that call for fancy white albacore.

MEYER LEMON SALSA
Makes 1½ cups

1 Meyer lemon (see Chef's Tip), plus fresh
    Meyer lemon juice to taste
6 shallots, minced
½ teaspoon salt, plus more to taste
¼ cup chopped fresh flat-leaf parsley
1 cup extra-virgin olive oil
Freshly ground pepper to taste

Cut the whole lemon, including the peel, into ⅛-inch-thick crosswise slices. Remove the seeds and cut the slices into ⅛-inch dice. Transfer the diced lemon to a mixing bowl. Add the shallots and salt and stir to combine the ingredients. Let sit at room temperature for 30 minutes.

Add the parsley and gradually whisk in the oil until thoroughly combined. Season with salt and pepper. Add additional lemon juice if desired.

Chef's Tip: Both the flesh and the rind of Meyer lemons are exceptionally sweet. If they are not available, organically grown lemons with sweet peels make an acceptable alternative. This salsa is ideal if you have your own Meyer lemon tree.

SHAVED VEGETABLE SALAD
Serves 6 as a salad course

DRESSING
1 tablespoon fresh lemon juice, or as needed
1 garlic clove, crushed
1 scant teaspoon champagne vinegar
Salt to taste
6 tablespoons extra-virgin olive oil, or as needed

3 large fennel bulbs, trimmed of stalks
    and halved from top to bottom
6 celery stalks
6 radishes
1 small summer squash
1 red or yellow pepper, seeded, deribbed,
    and cut into ½-inch strips
2 teaspoons fresh lemon juice (optional)
2 tablespoons olive oil
Salt and freshly ground pepper to taste
¼ cup chopped fresh flat-leaf parsley

To make the dressing: Combine the lemon juice, garlic, vinegar, and salt in a small bowl. Let sit at room temperature for 30 minutes. Gradually whisk in the oil until thoroughly combined. Taste and adjust the seasoning with salt.

No more than 2 hours before serving the salad, cut the vegetables into paper-thin slices with a sharp knife or a mandoline (see Chef's Tips). If not serving the salad immediately, toss the fennel with the optional lemon juice, seal in a plastic bag, and refrigerate; wrap the other shaved vegetables in a clean damp dish towel or napkin and refrigerate.

When ready to serve, toss all the shaved vegetables together in a bowl with the olive oil. Put them on chilled plates or a serving platter and sprinkle the vegetables with salt and pepper. Remove the garlic from the dressing and whisk it until thoroughly blended. Drizzle the dressing over the vegetables. Garnish the salad with parsley.

(continued on next page)

Chef's Tips: Other seasonal vegetables may be used, such as whole haricots verts, Romano beans, cucumbers, Belgian endive, or carrots.

The mandoline, named for the stroking motion the hand makes while using it, is an indispensable tool in most professional kitchens. The French model may be purchased in specialty cookware stores. An inexpensive Japanese version is found in Asian food markets. Exercise extreme caution when using this tool, as the blade is razor sharp.

ROASTED WILD MUSHROOMS WITH SHAVED PARMESAN
Serves 6

ROASTED MUSHROOMS

  12 ounces wild mushrooms, cleaned
    (such as cèpes, morels, and/or chanterelles;
    see Chef's Tips)
  ½ cup dry white wine
  2 tablespoons olive oil
  3 thyme sprigs
  Salt and freshly ground pepper to taste

DRESSING

  1 tablespoon minced shallots
  1 tablespoon balsamic vinegar
  1 tablespoon sherry vinegar
  ¼ teaspoon salt
  6 tablespoons olive oil, or as needed

  ¼ pound mixed greens
  Shaved Parmesan as needed (page 104)

To roast the mushrooms: Preheat the oven to 375°F. Cut the mushrooms into ½-inch-thick slices. Combine the mushrooms, wine, oil, thyme, salt, and pepper in a roasting pan large enough to hold the mushrooms in a single layer. Cover and roast for 30 to 40 minutes.

To make dressing: Combine the shallots, vinegars, and salt in a small bowl. Let sit at room temperature for 30 minutes. Gradually whisk in the oil until thoroughly combined.

Remove the roasting pan from the oven and pour off the cooking juices into a medium sauté pan. Return the pan to the oven and roast the mushrooms, uncovered, for 5 to 10 minutes, or until the edges begin to crisp (see Chef's Tips). Meanwhile, simmer the cooking juices over medium heat until reduced to a syrupy consistency.

To serve, combine the mixed greens with the dressing in a large bowl and toss until the greens are evenly coated. Serve the salad on salad plates and top with the roasted mushrooms (remove and discard the thyme sprigs). Drizzle the reduced cooking juices over the mushrooms and greens. Garnish the salad with Parmesan.

Chef's Tips: Mushrooms usually can be adequately cleaned by wiping them with a damp cloth or a soft brush. If they are extremely gritty, however, they may need to be rinsed. In that case, let them drain thoroughly before roasting. You may also need to increase the roasting time so that the excess water can cook away.

Cèpes (also known in Italian as porcini) may become bitter if they are allowed to become too brown during the final stage of roasting.

BASTILLE DAY
A COUNTRY FRENCH PICNIC

Certified Master Chef Fritz Sonnenschmidt

Bastille Day marks the anniversary of the beginning of the French Revolution in 1789. The commemoration of the country's quest for freedom remains a joyous holiday in France, where families use the occasion to gather for picnics and summer luncheons.

Only in America could a German by birth celebrate a French holiday. As a melting pot, it is not unusual for people from a variety of backgrounds to adopt the traditions of other cultures and embrace their spirit as their own. As a naturalized American citizen, I am honored to celebrate the universal principles of "Liberty, Equality and Fraternity" that Bastille Day has come to represent.

SMOKED SHRIMP WITH SAUCE LAMAZE
Serves 6 as an appetizer

MARINADE
1 cup dry white wine
⅓ cup olive oil
2 tablespoons grated orange zest
2 tablespoons minced fresh sage
2 garlic cloves, crushed
1½ teaspoons kosher salt
1 teaspoon peppercorns, crushed
1 teaspoon minced fresh rosemary

24 large shrimp, shelled and deveined
Olive oil for brushing
1 cup fine hickory or apple wood chips
Sauce Lamaze (recipe follows)

To make the marinade: Combine all the marinade ingredients in a small bowl. Cover and refrigerate overnight. Add the shrimp, cover, and let sit at room temperature for 1 hour.

Preheat a grill to high heat. Drain the shrimp and pat dry with paper towels. Lightly oil the shrimp and place them in a grill basket. Make a small tray out of aluminum foil to hold the wood chips. Place the tray of chips directly over the heating element or the hottest area of the coals. When the chips start to smoke, place the shrimp on the grill, close the lid, and smoke the shrimp for 3 minutes. Remove the tray of wood chips. Turn the shrimp (still in the grill basket) and grill on the second side 3 minutes longer, or until pink and cooked through.

Let the shrimp cool to room temperature. Serve with the sauce.

SAUCE LAMAZE
Makes 1¼ cups

½ cup mayonnaise
½ cup sour cream
2 to 3 tablespoons pickle relish
1 to 2 tablespoons ketchup
1 teaspoon minced fresh chervil or parsley

Combine all ingredients in a bowl and mix until thoroughly combined. Cover and refrigerate for at least 1 hour before serving

Chef's Tips: This sauce may be used as a dipping sauce, a cocktail sauce, or a salad dressing.

Sauce Lamaze may be stored, covered, in the refrigerator for up to 3 days.

LAMB STEAKS PROVENÇAL
Serves 6

MARINADE
½ cup dry white wine
½ cup olive oil
2 to 3 sage leaves
1 rosemary sprig
1 thyme sprig
½ teaspoon anise seed, or to taste
½ teaspoon ground cinnamon, or to taste

Six 8-ounce lamb steaks cut from the leg,
    each about 1 inch thick, trimmed
2 to 3 whole garlic bulbs
1 teaspoon olive oil
Pinch dried rosemary, crumbled
Pinch dried thyme, crumbled

To make the marinade: Combine all the marinade ingredients in a small bowl. Put the steaks in a shallow baking dish. Pour the marinade over the steaks, cover, and let marinate in the refrigerator for at least 1 hour or overnight.

Preheat the oven to 350°F. Cut the tips off of the garlic bulbs. Brush with olive oil and sprinkle with the rosemary and thyme. Wrap the garlic in aluminum foil and roast for 1 hour, or until the juices from the garlic are golden brown. Let cool.

While the garlic is roasting, preheat the grill to high heat. Remove the lamb steaks from the marinade and let them drain. Brush the steaks lightly with olive oil and grill them on one side for 4 minutes, or until a deep brown. Turn the steaks and grill another 3 to 4 minutes for a medium doneness. Adjust the cooking time to suit your personal preference for doneness.

To serve, place the steaks on a platter. Squeeze the roasted garlic over the steaks. Serve the steaks hot or at room temperature.

Chef's Tip: The steaks may be grilled up to 24 hours in advance, and kept, tightly wrapped, in the refrigerator. Remove them from the refrigerator or cooler 20 minutes before serving to take the chill off.

TOMATO AND OLIVE PIZZA
Serves 6

TOMATO SAUCE

    2 tablespoons olive oil
    1 onion, minced
    2 garlic cloves, minced
    ¼ cup ketchup
    4 plum tomatoes, peeled, seeded,
        and chopped, juices reserved (page 103)
    Pinch of saffron threads
    Herb bundle: ½ celery stalk, 1 thyme sprig,
        3 parsley stems, 1 tarragon sprig, and
        1 dill sprig, tied together (see Chef's Tips)
    Salt and freshly ground pepper to taste

    1 pound pizza dough (see Chef's Tips)
    2 large red peppers, roasted, peeled,
        and cut into ¼-inch-thick strips (page 104)
    1 cup black olives, pitted and slivered
    1 egg, beaten
    Olive oil as needed

To make the tomato sauce: Heat the olive oil in a medium sauté pan over medium heat. Add the onion and sauté, stirring frequently, for 3 to 5 minutes, or until limp. Add the garlic and stir until the aroma is released. Stir in the ketchup, tomatoes, and their juices. Add the saffron and the herb bundle. Cook over medium heat, stirring frequently, until the sauce has a syrupy consistency, about 15 to 20 minutes. Remove and discard the herb bundle, season to taste with salt and pepper, and set aside.

    Preheat the oven to 450°F. Butter a deep 12-inch tart pan. On a lightly floured work surface, roll out the dough to a 14-inch circle. Fit the dough into the tart pan and crimp the edges to form a rim.

Spread the tomato sauce evenly over surface of the dough and top with the pepper strips and olives. Brush the rim of the dough with the beaten egg. Bake for 20 to 30 minutes, or until the dough is light golden brown. (If the tomato mixture begins to look dry, cover the tart with aluminum foil.) Brush or drizzle the entire pizza lightly with olive oil. Serve hot or room temperature, cut into wedges.

Chef's Tips: To make the herb bundle, nestle the herbs in the hollow of the celery stalk. Secure tightly with cotton string.

The tomato sauce may be prepared in advance. Let it cool to room temperature, cover, and refrigerate for up to 2 days before using.

Pizza dough may be purchased from your favorite pizza shop, bakery, or supermarket. Or, use the flatbread dough on page 60.

RADISH SALAD WITH PEARS
Serves 6 as a side dish

36 small radishes, cut into very thin slices
2 pears, peeled, quartered,
    and cut into very thin slices
¼ cup distilled white vinegar
2 tablespoons olive oil
1 teaspoon sugar, or to taste
Salt and freshly ground pepper to taste
3 tablespoons plain yogurt

Combine the sliced radishes and pears in a large bowl. Add the vinegar, oil, sugar, salt, and pepper. Stir gently until well combined. Cover and marinate at room temperature for 15 minutes. Blend in the yogurt. Taste and adjust the seasoning. Cover and refrigerate for at least 1 to 2 hours before serving.

CHERRY CLAFOUTIS
Serves 6

4 cups fresh cherries, pitted
2 tablespoons kirschwasser

BATTER
4 eggs
6 tablespoons granulated sugar
Seeds from 1 vanilla bean (page 102)
Pinch of salt
1 tablespoon dark rum
1½ cups sifted all-purpose flour
1¾ cups milk

Powdered sugar for dusting

Combine the cherries and kirschwasser in a large bowl and let sit for 1 hour at room temperature.

To make the batter: Combine the eggs and sugar in a large bowl. Using a whisk or an electric mixer, beat the egg mixture until foamy. Mix in the vanilla seeds, salt, rum, and flour. Mix in the milk to form a smooth batter.

Preheat the oven to 350°F. Lightly butter a 13-inch oval ceramic baking dish. Pour about one third of the batter into the dish. Cover the batter with the cherries. Pour the remaining batter evenly over the cherries. Bake for about 30 minutes, or until a toothpick inserted near the center comes out clean.

Dust with powdered sugar. Serve hot, warm, or at room temperature.

Chef's Tip: Clafoutis originated in Alsace, a region of France noted for its cherries, but it is also made from other seasonal fruits, such as apples or pears. If apples are substituted for the cherries, replace the kirschwasser with an apple brandy or Calvados. If using pears, substitute pear brandy or eau-de-vie.

SUMMER SANDWICH SMORGASBORD

Certified Master Chef Fritz Sonnenschmidt

My Summer Sandwich Smorgasbord menu offers four styles of sandwiches: open-faced, full-sized, finger, and canapés. Whatever form you prefer, sandwiches are an ideal casual food for summer entertaining, because they are quick to prepare. They lend themselves to social gatherings because they can be eaten without knives and forks — in fact, fingers and napkins are all you need. I hope my unusual combinations will find a place in your own sandwich repertoire.

SMOKED TROUT SANDWICHES
Serves 4; makes 8 finger sandwiches

COTTAGE CHEESE MIXTURE
¼ cup cottage cheese
2 tablespoons ketchup
1 tablespoon oil
1 tablespoon balsamic vinegar
½ teaspoon ground pepper
½ teaspoon sugar
20 small cooked mushrooms, thinly sliced
8 green pimiento-stuffed olives, thinly sliced
1 tart green apple, peeled, cored and grated
¼ cup finely chopped pickled pearl onions

4 rye bread slices, halved diagonally
4 teaspoons butter at room temperature
4 smoked trout fillets, quartered
8 chervil or parsley sprigs

To make the cottage cheese mixture: Combine the cottage cheese, ketchup, oil, and vinegar in a small bowl. Add the pepper and sugar. Fold in the mushrooms, olives, apple, and onions until evenly blended. Set aside.

To assemble the sandwiches: Spread the bread with the butter. Top each piece of bread with 2 pieces of trout. Top the smoked trout with some of the cottage cheese mixture. Garnish each sandwich with a chervil or parsley sprig.

UKRAINIAN HAM AND KIELBASA SANDWICHES
Serves 4; makes 4 full-sized sandwiches

½ pound boiled ham, diced
½ pound kielbasa, diced
½ cup bread and butter pickles,
    drained and finely chopped
½ cup mayonnaise, or as needed
Salt and freshly ground pepper to taste
8 leaves Boston or Bibb lettuce
8 Russian pumpernickel bread slices

Combine the ham, kielbasa, and pickles in a meat grinder or a food processor and grind until evenly combined. (If you are using a food processor, pulse it on and off to avoid over-mixing.) Transfer to a small bowl, and add mayonnaise as needed to achieve a good spreading consistency. Season with salt and pepper.

Place 2 lettuce leaves on each of 4 slices of pumpernickel. Top with the ham mixture and top each sandwich with second slice of pumpernickel. Cut in half diagonally and serve.

Chef's Tip: A dark Bavarian beer is a good accompaniment to this sandwich.

VEGETARIAN SANDWICHES
Serves 4; makes 4 full-sized sandwiches

4 red potatoes
2 teaspoons olive oil
½ teaspoon caraway seeds
Salt and freshly ground pepper to taste
4 teaspoons mayonnaise
8 whole wheat bread slices
2 beefsteak tomatoes, sliced ¼ inch thick
4 tablespoons chopped olives
2 teaspoons balsamic vinegar, or to taste

Cook the potatoes in a medium saucepan of salted boiling water until tender, 15 to 20 minutes. Drain and let cool to the touch. Peel and cut the potatoes into ¼-inch-thick slices.

Heat the olive oil in a large sauté pan over medium heat. Add the potato slices in one layer and cook for 2 to 3 minutes on each side, or until they are golden brown. Sprinkle with the caraway seeds, salt, and pepper.

To assemble the sandwich: Spread some mayonnaise on one side of each bread slice. Top 4 of the bread slices with the potato, then the tomato slices. Sprinkle each sandwich with 1 tablespoon chopped olives and ½ teaspoon of the balsamic vinegar. Place a second slice of bread on top of each, cut the sandwiches in half diagonally, and serve.

BORSCHT SANDWICHES
Serves 4; makes 4 full-sized sandwiches

SOUR CREAM DRESSING
4 teaspoons sour cream
½ teaspoon caraway seeds
Salt and freshly ground pepper to taste

8 Russian pumpernickel bread slices
1 small red onion, thinly sliced
¼ cup cole slaw, drained (see Chef's Tips)
2 small pickled beets, thinly sliced (see Chef's Tips)
8 slices cooked roast beef or goose
Chopped fresh thyme to taste
2 dill pickles, halved lengthwise, for garnish

To make the dressing: Combine all the dressing ingredients in a small bowl and blend thoroughly.

To assemble the sandwich: Spread 4 of the pumpernickel slices with some of the sour cream dressing. Layer the pumpernickel with the red onion slices, cole slaw, beets, and roast beef or goose. Season with salt and pepper, scatter with thyme, and top with a second slice of pumpernickel.

Slice the pickle halves into fans and serve with the sandwiches.

Chef's Tips: Bottled pickled beets are available in most grocery stores (look in the dairy case). Or, use the Beet Preserves on page 9.

Use prepared cole slaw from your favorite deli, or prepare the version on page 51.

SUNDAY BRUNCH SANDWICHES
Serves 4; makes 4 full-sized sandwiches

CHICKEN BREASTS
4 small boneless, skinless chicken breast halves
Salt and freshly ground pepper to taste
½ teaspoon Hungarian paprika
3 tablespoons olive oil

CURRIED SCRAMBLED EGGS
4 eggs
3 tablespoons chopped fresh dill
2 teaspoons Madras curry
Salt and freshly ground pepper to taste
2 tablespoons unsalted butter
¼ cup finely diced red pepper

8 white bread slices
4 teaspoons mayonnaise
4 lettuce leaves
4 dill sprigs

To prepare the chicken: Season the chicken breasts with salt, pepper, and paprika. Heat the olive oil in a large sauté pan over medium heat. Add the chicken and sauté for 5 minutes on each side, or until opaque throughout and springy to the touch. Transfer the chicken to a plate and keep it warm while preparing the scrambled eggs.

To prepare the eggs: Beat the eggs, dill, curry, salt, and pepper in a medium bowl. Melt the butter in a 10-inch sauté pan over medium heat. Add the red pepper and sauté until limp, about 3 minutes. Reduce heat to low. Pour in the egg mixture and stir until the eggs are just set, about 1 to 2 minutes.

To assemble the sandwiches: Toast the bread and spread one side of each piece with some of the mayonnaise. Top each toast slice with a lettuce leaf. Slice each chicken breast into ¼-inch-thick diagonal slices and place on the lettuce. Divide the curried eggs among the sandwiches and top with a second piece of toast. Cut the sandwiches in half diagonally. Serve on warm plates, garnished with dill sprigs.

HAM PATTY SANDWICHES
Serves 4; makes 4 open-faced sandwiches

12 ounces Westphalian ham or prosciutto, ground
4 ounces ground pork
¼ cup dried breadcrumbs
3 tablespoons milk
2 eggs
2 teaspoons lightly packed brown sugar
2 canned pineapple slices, halved
4 rye bread slices
4 teaspoons cream cheese
1 teaspoon minced olives
4 lettuce leaves
4 mint sprigs

Preheat the oven to 400°F. Combine the ham and pork in a meat grinder or a food processor and grind until evenly combined. (If you are using a food processor, pulse it on and off to avoid overmixing.) Combine the bread crumbs, milk, eggs, and brown sugar in a medium bowl and mix well. Add the ground ham and pork to the bread crumb mixture and stir until evenly blended.

Mold the ham mixture into 4 patties and place in a baking dish. Top each patty with a piece of pineapple. Bake for 5 to 7 minutes, or until the patty is opaque throughout or registers 150°F on an instant-read thermometer.

To assemble the sandwich: Toast the bread. Mix the cream cheese and olives and spread on the rye toast. Top each piece of toast with a lettuce leaf and a ham patty. Garnish with mint sprigs and serve warm.

PORK TENDERLOIN SMØRREBRØD
Serves 4; makes 4 smørrebrød

Four 3-ounce pork tenderloin medallions
1 cup vegetable oil
Salt and freshly ground pepper to taste
2 potatoes, thinly sliced (see Chef's Tips)
¼ cup mayonnaise
1 tablespoon chopped fresh dill
4 white bread slices
4 small tomatoes, peeled, quartered,
    and seeded (page 103)
4 watercress sprigs

Preheat a grill to high heat. Brush the medallions with a little of the oil and season well with salt and pepper. Grill the medallions for 3 to 4 minutes on each side, or until an instant-read thermometer inserted in the pork registers 150°F. Let the medallions cool to room temperature.

Heat the remaining oil in a medium, heavy saucepan over medium heat to 375°F, or until almost smoking (see Chef's Tip). Add the potato slices and fry until crisp, about 5 to 7 minutes. Using a slotted spoon, transfer the potato chips to paper towels to drain and sprinkle them lightly with salt.

To assemble the smørrebrød: Toast the bread slices. Mix the mayonnaise and dill and place a spoonful in the center of each piece of toast. Arrange 4 tomato quarters and some potato chips around the mayonnaise and top with a pork medallion. Garnish with a watercress sprigs.

Chef's Tips: Prepared potato chips may be substituted for the homemade chips.

To check to see if the oil is hot enough, add a cube of bread. It should become golden in about 60 seconds.

SWEET AND SAVORY SUMMER FRUITS

Chef Bill Reynolds and
Certified Master Pastry Chef Markus Färbinger

This selection of sweet and savory summer fruits showcases the wide range of dishes you can prepare from fruit. You can use vinegar and spice to flavor a fruit dish, or you can use fruits and herbs to flavor vinegar. In addition, our Fusion Gazpacho, made from a blend of vegetables and fruits, shows how just changing the cut of the ingredients can transform this dish from a salad to a salsa to a soup.

The natural sweetness of fruits makes them obvious choices for the dessert menu. The classic Peach Melba, originally prepared by August Escoffier in honor of the famed diva Dame Melba, pairs peaches with a luscious raspberry sauce. The mysterious wild strawberry biscuit omelet is sure to delight even those who normally pass up desserts.

PEACH AND ROSEMARY VINEGAR
Makes 4 cups

2 large ripe peaches, peeled, pitted,
    and cut into ¾-inch dice
4 cups cider vinegar
5 rosemary sprigs

Combine the peaches and vinegar in a blender or food processor and pulse for 5 seconds. (Do not over-blend.) Transfer to a clean glass jar. Cover tightly and let stand at room temperature overnight. Strain the mixture through a fine-meshed sieve. Transfer to a clean jar and add the rosemary sprigs. Cover and store in the refrigerator for up to 6 months.

PICKLED PEACHES OR FIGS
Makes 12 figs or peach halves (about 4 cups)

6 peaches, peeled, pitted, and halved
    –or–12 fresh whole figs
8 cups sugar
4 cups cider vinegar
2 cinnamon sticks

Place the peaches or figs in a large bowl. Combine the remaining ingredients in a large saucepan and bring to a boil over high heat and pour it over the fruit. Cover and refrigerate for at least 8 hours before using.

Chef's Tips: To store, drain the fruit, put it in a clean, covered container, and refrigerate for up to 1 week.
Serve with ham, grilled chicken, or grilled or roasted pork.

FUSION GAZPACHO:
A SALAD, SALSA, OR SOUP
Serves 4 as a salad course

DRESSING
½ cup Chicken Broth (page 107)
½ teaspoon saffron threads
1 jalapeño chili, seeded and minced
Juice and grated zest of 2 limes
2 tablespoons minced fresh cilantro
1 cup virgin olive oil
Salt to taste

SALAD
2 large red tomatoes, peeled (page 103)
2 large yellow tomatoes, peeled (page 103)
2 tomatillos, cut into 1-inch chunks
½ cup thinly sliced peeled cucumber
½ cup cantaloupe balls cut with a melon baller
½ cup large chunks seeded watermelon (about 1 inch)
½ cup medium dice mango
¼ cup thinly sliced peeled chayote
1 small red onion, cut into small dice
¼ cup medium dice jícama
¼ cup medium dice red pepper

To make the dressing: Combine the chicken broth and saffron in a small pan and bring to a boil over medium heat. Remove from heat, and add the jalapeño, lime juice, and zest. Let cool to room temperature. Add the cilantro and gradually whisk in the olive oil until thoroughly combined. Set aside.

To make the salad: Put all the salad ingredients in a large bowl. Add the dressing and toss well. Refrigerate for 2 to 3 hours before serving.

Chef's Tips: To make salsa: Omit the salad dressing. Cut all the salad ingredients into small dice and add 2 tablespoons minced fresh cilantro and 1 minced jalapeño. Makes about 6 cups salsa.

To make soup: Prepare the dressing. Purée half of the salsa in a blender. Pour the purée into a bowl and add the remaining diced salsa ingredients and the dressing. Cover and refrigerate for 2 to 3 hours before serving. Serves 6; makes about 6 cups

POACHED PEACHES OR APRICOTS IN LEMON-VANILLA SYRUP
Makes about 8 cups fruit in syrup

3 pounds peaches or apricots

SYRUP
2 cups water
¾ cup sugar
Juice of 1 lemon, plus rind of ½ lemon
2 vanilla beans

Bring a large saucepan of water to a rolling boil over high heat. Drop a few peaches or apricots at a time into the boiling water for 30 seconds. Using a slotted spoon, transfer the fruit to a bowl of ice water until cool to the touch. Peel, remove the pit, and cut in half.

To make the syrup: Combine all the syrup ingredients in a large saucepan over medium heat. Bring the mixture to a boil and cook for 5 minutes.

Add the peach or apricot halves to the syrup and poach over medium heat until the peaches or apricots are cooked through (15 to 20 minutes for peaches; 6 to 8 minutes for apricots). Let the fruit cool in the syrup to room temperature. Remove the lemon rind and discard; the vanilla bean should remain in the syrup. Store the fruit in the syrup in a clean, covered container for up to 10 days in the refrigerator.

Chef's Tip: These poached peaches or apricots may be used in many recipes that call for poached or canned peaches. They may be canned for longer storage. Consult a canning guide for instructions regarding sterilization, hot-pack method, and appropriate processing times.

PEACH MELBA
Serves 8

RASPBERRY SAUCE
2 pints fresh raspberries
½ cup sugar
Juice of 2 lemons
2 tablespoons kirschwasser

8 Poached Peaches in Lemon-Vanilla Syrup, drained (see recipe this page)
2 pints vanilla ice cream
Whipped cream as needed
2 tablespoons sliced almonds, toasted (page 104)

To make the sauce: Combine the raspberries and sugar in a blender and purée until smooth. Stir in the lemon juice and kirschwasser and set aside.

To assemble: Place ¼ cup of the raspberry sauce in each of 8 champagne saucers. Place a peach half, flat-side up, in each champagne saucer. Place a scoop of ice cream on top of each peach half. Top with whipped cream and garnish with almonds. (See Chef's Tip.) Serve at once.

Chef's Tip: A nice addition to this dessert is a thin, wafer-style cookie. Purchased cookies or homemade versions add a bit of texture contrast to this classic and much-loved dessert.

BISCUIT OMELET
WITH WILD STRAWBERRIES
Serves 8

BISCUIT OMELET
  ½ cup plus 2 tablespoons granulated sugar
  4 egg yolks
  6 eggs
  1¼ cups cake flour, sifted

FILLING
  4 pints fresh wild strawberries, hulled
    (see Chef's Tips)
  1 cup heavy cream
  Powdered sugar to taste

To make the biscuit omelet: Preheat the oven to 450°F. Trace eight 5-inch circles on sheets of parchment paper and line baking sheets with the paper. Combine the sugar, egg yolks, and eggs in a double boiler over barely simmering water and heat, whisking constantly, until frothy and warm (95 to 100F° on an instant-read thermometer). Transfer the mixture to a large bowl. Using a whisk or an electric mixer, beat the mixture until it is cool, about 10 minutes. Gently fold in the flour. Transfer the mixture to a pastry bag fitted with a ⅜-inch-wide tip. Pipe the mixture in a spiral onto the parchment paper, completely filling each circle.

Bake the biscuit omelets for 4 minutes, or until the center of an omelet springs back when gently pressed with a fingertip. Remove them from the oven and slide the omelets, still on the parchment, onto a cold table or counter. Immediately cover with a clean cloth and let cool slightly.

To assemble: Using an electric mixer or a whisk, beat the cream until soft peaks form. Whisk in powdered sugar. Place strawberries on one half of each biscuit omelet and top with whipped cream. Fold each biscuit over to enclose the berries. Dust with powdered sugar. Serve warm.

Chef's Tips: Other seasonal berries may be used as a substitute for the wild strawberries.

You may burn a "tattoo" into each omelet using a special burnishing iron available in specialty cookware shops.

LATE-SUMMER VEGETABLES

Certified Master Chef Ron De Santis

As a child I spent each summer playing all day in my grandfather's garden. Maybe that's why cooking fresh vegetables from the garden feels so natural to me as a chef.

Grilling is a cooking method often overlooked for vegetables. It's especially effective for tender, juicy vegetables that can withstand the high, quick, intense heat of the grill. Mushrooms are also excellent grilled, as they take on an almost meatlike flavor.

The grilled vegetable ragout is my favorite way to use up all those vegetables I have in abundance and have been taking for granted all summer: zucchini, yellow squash, onions, tomatoes, and peppers. It's my way of celebrating summer's "last hurrah."

CAPELLINI WITH GRILLED VEGETABLE RAGOUT
Serves 5

1 red onion, cut into ¾-inch-thick slices
1 large zucchini, cut lengthwise
    into ¾-inch-thick slices
1 large yellow squash, cut lengthwise
    into ¾-inch-thick slices
1 fennel bulb, trimmed of stalks and quartered
1½ cups White Balsamic Vinaigrette (recipe follows)
2 garlic cloves, minced
Salt and freshly ground pepper to taste
1 pound dried capellini (angel hair) pasta
2 tomatoes, peeled, seeded and chopped (page 103)
1 *each* red, green, and yellow pepper,
    roasted, peeled, and cut into large dice (page 104)
1½ cups Vegetable Broth, plus more if needed
    (page 109)
2 tablespoons chopped fresh basil
1 tablespoon chopped fresh marjoram
2 tablespoons chopped fresh flat-leaf parsley

GARNISH
    5 flat-leaf parsley sprigs
    Shaved Parmesan (page 104),
        or 5 tablespoons grated Parmesan

In a shallow baking dish, toss together the onion, zucchini, squash, fennel, vinaigrette, garlic, salt, and pepper. Let sit for 30 minutes.

Preheat a grill to medium heat. Drain the vegetables from the marinade, reserving the marinade. Grill the vegetables until tender, turning once. The onions will take 3 to 6 minutes on each side; the zucchini and yellow squash, 4 to 5 minutes on each side; and the fennel, 10 to 12 minutes on each side. This may be done in batches if necessary. Allow the vegetables to cool before cutting them into large dice.

(continued on next page)

Cook the pasta in a large pot of salted boiling water until al dente, about 3 to 4 minutes. Drain, toss with extra-virgin olive oil, and keep warm.

Place the grilled vegetables, reserved marinade, chopped tomatoes, and roasted peppers in a large saucepan. Stir in the vegetable broth and simmer over medium heat until hot. Add the basil, marjoram, flat-leaf parsley, salt, and pepper. Add the pasta and toss until thoroughly combined and heated through. Add more vegetable broth if needed to give the dish a stewlike consistency.

To serve, mound the ragout and pasta on a warmed serving platter or individual plates. Garnish with parsley sprigs and shaved or grated Parmesan. Serve at once.

Chef's Tip: Capellini pasta may be found at Italian markets or specialty foods stores. If it is not available, use spaghettini.

TUSCAN BEAN SALAD
Serve 5; makes about 3 cups

2 cups drained cooked white beans (page 103)
1 large carrot, cut into small dice
2 celery stalks, cut into small dice
¼ cup snipped fresh chives
¼ cup minced fresh parsley
2 tablespoons *each* small dice green,
    red, and yellow pepper
1½ cups White Balsamic Vinaigrette
Salt and freshly ground pepper to taste

Combine all the ingredients in a medium bowl. Stir to thoroughly combine all the vegetables with the vinaigrette. Cover and marinate in the refrigerator for at least 2 hours. Taste and adjust the seasoning if necessary.

GRILLED PORTOBELLOS AND PROSCIUTTO WITH TUSCAN BEAN SALAD
Serves 5

5 portobello mushrooms, stemmed
    (about 4 inches in diameter)
2½ tablespoons olive oil
5 thin prosciutto slices
Tuscan Bean Salad
½ cup celery juice (see Chef's Tip)
1 tablespoon coarsely chopped fresh cilantro
¼ head radicchio, finely shredded

Preheat a grill to medium heat. Brush the portobellos with the olive oil and wrap each portobello cap with a slice of the prosciutto, leaving the gills unwrapped. Grill for 5 to 6 minutes on the gill side, or until tender. Turn the caps and grill for about 1 minute, or until the prosciutto crisps.

To serve, spoon bean salad onto each plate and pour some celery juice around the beans. Cut the portobellos into diagonal slices and arrange around the bean salad. Garnish with the cilantro and radicchio.

Chef's Tip: Celery juice may be made in a household juicer or purchased fresh or in bottles at natural foods stores.

WHITE BALSAMIC VINAIGRETTE
Makes 3 cups

¾ cup white balsamic vinegar (see Chef's Tip)
2¼ cups extra-virgin olive oil
Salt and freshly ground pepper to taste

Pour the vinegar into a medium bowl and gradually whisk in the oil until thoroughly combined. Season with salt and pepper.

Chef's Tip: White balsamic vinegar, also known as "sweet wine vinegar," is available at specialty foods markets and some supermarkets.

SUMMER STEW AU PISTOU
Serves 5

3 cups water, or as needed
One ¼-inch-thick slice (1 ounce) pancetta
¼ cup pinto beans, soaked (page 102)
¼ cup navy beans, soaked (page 102)
1 large carrot, cut into medium dice
1 Idaho potato, cut into medium dice
1 small onion, cut into medium dice
3 green onions, green and white portions,
    cut into ⅓-inch lengths

PISTOU
  2 plum tomatoes peeled, seeded,
    and chopped (page 103)
  ¼ bunch basil, leaves only, coarsely chopped
  2 tablespoons olive oil
  1 garlic clove, chopped
  Salt and freshly ground pepper to taste

3 tablespoons small dried pasta
    (shells, bow ties, or orrechietti)
¾ cup medium dice zucchini
1 cup green beans, cut into ¼-inch lengths
    and blanched (page 103)

Combine the water and pancetta in a large soup pot. Bring to a boil, reduce heat to a low simmer, and add the beans, carrot, potato, onion, and green onions. Cook for 1½ hours, or until the beans are very tender.

While the stew cooks, make the pistou: Combine all the pistou ingredients in a blender and purée to a smooth paste. Add a small amount of the stew liquid to adjust the consistency if necessary.

Add the pasta and zucchini to the cooking beans and cook for 5 minutes longer. Remove the piece of pancetta (see Chef's Tip). Stir the pistou and green beans into the stew and let stand at least 10 minutes before serving. Serve at once in warmed soup plates.

Chef's Tip: The pancetta is too good to be discarded. Try this "cook's bonus" atop a slice of crusty baguette and serve yourself a glass of hearty red wine to wash it down.

MARINATED GRILLED LAMB CHOPS
Serves 5

¼ cup balsamic vinegar
1½ tablespoons olive oil
2 thyme sprigs
2 rosemary sprigs
10 to 15 loin or rib lamb chops (3 to 5 ounces each)

Pour the vinegar and olive oil into a shallow container large enough to hold the chops in a single layer. Add the thyme and rosemary. Place the chops in the marinade and turn to coat them evenly. Marinate in the refrigerator for 30 minutes.

Preheat a grill to high heat. Grill the chops for 3 to 4 minutes on each side for medium-rare, or adjust the time for your preferred doneness.

LABOR-FREE
LABOR DAY COOKING

Chef Wayne Almquist and
Certified Master Pastry Chef Markus Färbinger

At first, Labor Day was observed as an important day for labor unions with meetings, union parades, and the like. Today, it is a more relaxed affair, with picnics and cookouts that signify the end to summer fun and a return to more serious pursuits in work and school.

This Labor Day menu includes a cold soup you can easily transport in a thermos. A peach chutney and cole slaw with apple are fabulous accompaniments to the cold pork chops. Crushed peanuts mixed into the bread crumb coating help retain a crunchy texture while adding a unique flavor. The passion fruit and raspberry tart transports safely in the tart mold and makes an elegant picnic dessert.

Say farewell to summer and welcome fall with our recipes that can easily be prepared in advance and enjoyed effortlessly at an outdoor party. Why work on Labor Day?

COLE SLAW WITH APPLE
Serves 8 as a side dish

3 cups thinly sliced green cabbage
2 cups thinly sliced red cabbage
3 green onions, green and white portions, thinly sliced
1 *each* green and red pepper, seeded, deribbed, and cut into medium dice
1 carrot, shredded
1 apple, peeled, cored, and thinly sliced

DRESSING
½ cup mayonnaise
½ cup sour cream
¼ cup thinly sliced green onion
2 tablespoons red wine vinegar
2 tablespoons maple syrup
1 tablespoon vegetable oil
1 tablespoon Dijon mustard
1 tablespoon poppy seeds
2 teaspoons fresh lemon juice
Kosher salt and freshly ground pepper to taste

Combine the cabbages, green onions, peppers, carrot, and apple in a large bowl and toss.

To make the dressing: Combine all the dressing ingredients and mix well. Pour the dressing over the cabbage mixture and toss well to blend. Cover and refrigerate for 1 hour before serving.

Chef's Tip: The vegetables may be cut and the dressing made 1 day in advance. Refrigerate the vegetables in a sealed plastic bag. Cover and refrigerate the dressing. About 1 hour before serving, slice the apple, add it to the vegetables, and toss the salad with the dressing.

COLD TOMATO AND ZUCCHINI SOUP
Serves 6 as a soup course

1¼ pounds plum tomatoes, peeled, seeded,
   and coarsely chopped (about 4 cups), page 103
2 cups tomato juice
1 small onion, coarsely chopped
1 red pepper, seeded, deribbed, and coarsely chopped
½ cucumber, peeled, seeded, and coarsely chopped
½ zucchini, coarsely chopped
¼ cup chopped fresh cilantro
¼ cup chopped fresh basil
¼ cup chopped fresh parsley
1½ tablespoons drained, prepared horseradish
   (or use recipe on page 9)
1 tablespoon red wine vinegar
3 garlic cloves, chopped
Chicken Broth, if needed (page 107)
Tabasco sauce to taste
Salt and freshly ground pepper to taste
Seasoned Croutons for garnish (page 104)

Combine all the ingredients except the broth, Tabasco, salt, and pepper in a blender or food processor, working in batches if necessary. Process the soup in short pulses to a coarse purée. Pour the soup into a bowl. If it is too thick, thin it slightly with chicken broth. Add the Tabasco, salt, and pepper. Refrigerate for at least 30 minutes before serving. Garnish with croutons.

PEANUT-CRUSTED PORK CHOPS WITH FRESH PEACH CHUTNEY
Serves 8 as a main course

4 eggs
¼ cup vegetable oil
3 tablespoons peanut butter
2¾ cups dry bread crumbs
1¾ cups (8 ounces) honey-roasted peanuts,
   finely ground
Eight 6-ounce pork chops
Salt and freshly ground pepper to taste
½ cup flour, or as needed for dredging
½ cup olive oil, or as needed for frying
½ cup clarified butter, or as needed for frying
   (page 104)
Fresh Peach Chutney (recipe follows)

Combine the eggs, oil, and peanut butter in a small bowl and whisk until thoroughly combined. Combine the bread crumbs and ground peanuts in a shallow bowl.

Season the pork chops with salt and pepper. Dredge the chops in the flour, shaking off any excess. Dip the chops in the egg mixture, then in the bread crumb mixture, making sure each chop is completely coated.

Add equal amounts of oil and butter to a large cast-iron skillet to a depth of ¼ inch. Heat over medium-high heat until the mixture shimmers slightly. Add the pork chops in a single layer. Cook on the first side for 5 minutes, turn, and cook another 5 minutes, or until the chops are firm to the touch and completely cooked through. Drain on paper towels. Add additional oil and butter if necessary to cook the remaining pork chops. Let the chops cool to room temperature, then cover and refrigerate until ready to serve.

Serve the cold chops with fresh peach chutney.

FRESH PEACH CHUTNEY
Serves 8; makes about 4 cups

6 ripe peaches, peeled, pitted,
    and cut into medium dice (about 2½ cups)
⅓ cup *each* finely diced red and green pepper
½ cup dried currants, plumped in warm water
    for 30 minutes
⅓ cup chopped walnuts
2 tablespoons lightly packed brown sugar
2 tablespoons ground coriander
1 tablespoon fresh lime juice
2 teaspoons minced jalapeño chili, or to taste

Combine all the ingredients in large bowl and toss gently until thoroughly combined. Cover and refrigerate overnight.

Chef's Tip: Sprinkle the chutney with a few drops of peach liqueur just prior to serving if you wish.

FLAVORED BUTTER
Makes about 1¼ cups

1 cup (2 sticks) unsalted butter, cut into pieces
¼ cup chopped roasted red pepper (page 104)
2 tablespoons minced jalapeño chili
½ tablespoon Dijon mustard

Combine all the ingredients in a food processor and pulse until blended. Spread the butter onto a piece of plastic wrap or waxed paper. Fold the plastic over the butter and roll to form a 1- to 2-inch-diameter log. Press against the butter with heel of knife to firm it up. Twist the ends of the plastic tightly. Refrigerate the butter until firm. When ready to use, slice into ¼-inch-thick coins, remove the plastic, and place on hot food.

Chef's Tips: This butter is excellent served with grilled corn or other grilled vegetables.

For a basil variation, replace the jalapeño, pepper, and mustard with 2 tablespoons chopped fresh basil and 1 tablespoon fresh lemon juice.

For a garlic variation, combine the butter with the purée from 1 head of roasted garlic (page 103).

PASSION FRUIT AND RASPBERRY TART
Serves 8 to 10; makes one 12-inch tart

One 12-inch prebaked Tart Shell (page 109)
2 ounces dark chocolate, melted
1 layer Chocolate Sponge Cake (page 110)
⅓ cup seedless raspberry jam

PASSION FRUIT CREAM
1 cup milk
2 tablespoons sugar
¼ cup cornstarch
3 egg yolks
¼ cup passion fruit juice (page 105)

MERINGUE
½ cup water
1 cup plus 2 tablespoons sugar
4 egg whites
1 tablespoon chocolate extract

2 pints fresh raspberries
Powdered sugar for dusting
⅓ cup sliced almonds, toasted (page 104)

Brush the tart shell with the melted chocolate. Add the chocolate sponge cake layer and spread it with the jam.

To make the cream: Combine the milk and half of the sugar in a medium saucepan. Bring to a boil over medium heat. While the milk is heating, combine the cornstarch and the remaining 1 tablespoon sugar in a small bowl. Add the egg yolks and ¼ cup of the hot milk and whisk thoroughly. Pour the yolk mixture back into the milk mixture in the saucepan. Cook, stirring constantly, until the cream returns to a boil and thickens. Remove the cream from heat and stir in the passion fruit juice. Let the passion fruit cream cool to room temperature and refrigerate it until ready to assemble the tart.

To make the meringue: Combine the water and 1 cup of the sugar in a small saucepan. Stir lightly. Bring to a boil over high heat and cook for 2 to 3 minutes, until it registers 240°F, or a small amount dropped in a glass of water forms a soft pliable ball. Remove from heat and cover the pan with a lid.

While the sugar is cooking, beat the egg whites and the 2 tablespoons sugar and chocolate extract in a large bowl with an electric mixer until soft peaks form. (Continue beating the eggs on low speed until the sugar is ready, if necessary.)

When the sugar is the correct temperature, beat the whites on high speed until stiff peaks form. Reduce the speed to low and pour the hot syrup slowly into the whipped whites, letting the syrup fall in between the whip and the side of the bowl. Whip until the meringue is cool.

To assemble the tart: Preheat the oven to 450°F. Fold the passion fruit cream together with half of the meringue. Place the raspberries in a single layer in the tart shell, reserving 12 berries for garnish, and top with the passion fruit cream. Spread the remaining meringue over the cream. Dust the entire surface with the powdered sugar and scatter with almonds.

Brown the tart in the oven for 1 minute. Garnish with the reserved berries. Let the tart cool completely before slicing with a serrated knife.

Chef's Tips: Use the teeth of a serrated knife or a cake decorating comb to spread the meringue evenly as well as to give the tart a decorative finish. If you have a blowtorch, you can use it to very quickly brown the meringue. However, a hot oven works well.

To vary the tart's flavor, replace the passion fruit juice with fresh lemon, lime, red currant, or other tart fruit juices.

If you wish to simplify the tart, you can opt to leave out the cake layer.

COOKING FOR ROSH HASHANAH

Chef Morey Kanner

Our cooking series ends with a menu for a holiday that represents a beginning: Rosh Hashanah, the Jewish New Year. It is the first day of the month of Tishiri, and begins ten days of penitence that end with Yom Kippur, the day of atonement. The menu of kreplach, tzimmes, lamb shank, and potato kugel are very much a part of my family's annual tradition.

Pastry Chef Stacy Radin

For Rosh Hashanah it is customary to serve something "sweet," in the hope that "sweetness" will last for the whole year. It is this symbolism of the honey cake that makes it a traditional Rosh Hashanah treat.

After extensive testing in search of the quintessential honey cake, I came across a collection of recipes from Israel including what is certainly one of the best honey cakes I've ever tried adapted here with some slight adjustments in flavoring.

BEEF DUMPLINGS WITH CHICKEN BROTH
KREPLACH
Serves 8 as a soup course

2 tablespoons chicken fat, melted
   (reserved from chicken broth)
2 tablespoons minced garlic
2 tablespoons grated fresh ginger
¼ cup minced green onions, green
   and white portions
1 pound lean ground beef
Salt and freshly ground pepper to taste
24 wonton wrappers (see Chef's Tips)
1 egg, beaten
8 cups Chicken Broth (page 107), heated

To make the kreplach: Heat the chicken fat in a medium sauté pan over medium heat. Add the garlic, ginger and green onions and sauté for 15 to 30 seconds, or until the aroma is released. Add the ground beef and cook for about 5 minutes, or until meat loses its redness and the juices have cooked away. Season with salt and pepper. Spread the meat mixture onto a baking sheet and refrigerate until completely chilled.

Lay out the wonton wrappers on a work surface. Place 1 tablespoon of the cooled meat mixture on each of the wrappers. Brush the edges of a wrapper with the beaten egg and fold to form a triangle. Seal the edges, pressing out any air pockets. Repeat with the remaining wonton wrappers until all the wrappers are sealed.

Bring a large pot of salted water to a boil. Reduce the heat to a simmer, add the wontons and cook for 2 minutes, or until the wonton wrappers are tender. Using a slotted spoon, transfer the kreplach to warmed soup bowls. Season the broth with salt and pepper. Ladle the broth over the kreplach and serve.

Chef's Tips: A nice addition to the soup would be diced cooked chicken, cooked sliced shiitake mushrooms, and cooked julienned autumn vegetables such as rutabagas, parsnip, and carrot.

Wonton wrappers can be bought in many supermarkets in the produce section or at Asian markets. If frozen, thaw them before using.

AUTUMN VEGETABLES AND DRIED FRUIT
TZIMMES
Serves 8 as a side dish

1 tablespoon pearl barley
2 cups water
⅓ cup lightly packed brown sugar
½ cinnamon stick
Pinch freshly grated nutmeg
2 cups large dice carrots, pumpkin or winter squash
¼ cup large dice dried apricots
2 dried Black Mission figs, cut into large dice
¼ cup dried cherries
4 pitted prunes, cut into large dice
¼ cup golden raisins
¼ teaspoon salt

Combine the barley, water, sugar, cinnamon stick, and nutmeg in a medium saucepan. Cook over medium heat for 30 to 45 minutes, or until the barley is completely cooked. Add all the remaining ingredients and continue simmering for 10 to 15 minutes, or until the vegetables are tender but not mushy. Add a little more water if necessary during the cooking. Served hot, at room temperature, or cold.

Chef's Tip: This dish has a better consistency if it is made the day before you plan to serve it.

BRAISED LAMB SHANKS
WITH BARLEY, ONIONS, AND ALE
Serves 8 as a main course

8 lamb shanks
¼ cup olive oil
Salt and freshly ground pepper to taste
12 ounces pearl onions, peeled
8 garlic cloves, slivered
Four 12-ounce bottles amber ale
4 cups Chicken Broth (page 107)
¼ cup Dijon mustard
½ cup balsamic vinegar
¼ cup molasses
½ cup pearl barley
1 parsnip, cut into medium dice
1 carrot, cut into medium dice
1 cup medium dice celery root
1 cup medium dice rutabaga
Thyme sprigs for garnish

Preheat the oven to 400°F. Coat the shanks with the oil and season with salt and pepper. Place the shanks in a roasting pan or Dutch oven large enough to hold them in a single layer. Roast, uncovered, for 20 to 30 minutes, or until the shanks are deep brown, but not burned. Remove the shanks from the pan and set aside.

Pour off most of the fat from the pan and place over medium heat. Add the pearl onions and sauté for 8 to 10 minutes, or until golden brown. Add the garlic and sauté for 1 minute. Pour in 2 bottles of the ale and stir to loosen the pan drippings. Simmer for 3 minutes, then add the remaining 2 bottles of ale, the broth, mustard, vinegar, and molasses. Bring to a boil and add the shanks, plus any juices they may have released, to the pan. Spread the shanks out into one layer.

(continued on next page)

Reduce the oven temperature to 350°F. Cover the pan with a lid or aluminum foil and put in the oven. Braise the shanks for 1 hour. Stir in the barley and turn the shanks over. Cover the pan and braise the shanks for 45 more minutes. Add the parsnip, carrot, celery root, and rutabaga and cook, covered, for another 10 to 15 minutes, or until the vegetables are tender and the lamb is almost falling off the bone. Spoon any excess fat from the surface of the sauce. Taste and adjust the seasoning with salt and pepper.

To serve, place the shanks on a warmed serving platter or plates and spoon the vegetables and sauce over them. Garnish with thyme sprigs.

POTATO KUGEL WITH PARSNIPS AND LEEKS
Serves 8 as a side dish

6 yellow potatoes, peeled and cut into large dice
3 parsnips, peeled and cut into large dice
¼ cup rendered chicken fat (see Chef's Tip)
1 onion, grated
1 leek, white part only, cut into small dice (page 103)
3 large eggs, beaten
½ cup matzo meal
½ cup water or Chicken Broth (page 107)
1 teaspoon baking powder
Salt and freshly ground pepper to taste
Pinch freshly grated nutmeg

Cook the potatoes and parsnips separately in salted boiling water for 10 to 12 minutes, or until very tender. Drain thoroughly and combine in a large bowl. Using a ricer or potato masher, rice or mash the potatoes and parsnips until they form a smooth purée.

Preheat the oven to 350°F. Heat the chicken fat in a medium sauté pan over medium heat. Add the onion and leek and sauté for 8 to 10 minutes, or until lightly browned. Transfer to a plate and let cool completely.

Add the onion mixture to the vegetables. Add the eggs, matzo meal, water, and baking powder and blend well. Add the salt, pepper, and nutmeg. Put the mixture into a well-greased 8-inch square baking dish. Bake for 20 to 30 minutes, or until the top is nicely browned. Serve hot.

Chef's Tip: Chicken fat (schmaltz) may be purchased (look for it in your dairy case), or you can reserve it from the homemade Chicken Broth (page 107).

HONEY CAKE
Makes two 8-by-4-inch loaf cakes

3½ cups all-purpose flour
4 teaspoons baking powder
1 teaspoon ground allspice
1 teaspoon ground cinnamon
¼ teaspoon ground ginger
Pinch of salt
4 eggs
1 cup tightly packed brown sugar
1½ cups golden honey
1 cup strong brewed coffee
2 teaspoons vegetable oil
Juice and grated zest of 1 orange
Grated zest of 1 lemon
Sweetened whipped cream with ground cinnamon
     to taste (optional)

Preheat the oven to 325°F. Sift the flour, baking powder, allspice, cinnamon, ginger, and salt together in a medium a bowl.

Combine the eggs and sugar in a large bowl and beat until blended using an electric hand mixer. Add the honey, coffee, oil, orange juice, and zests. Mix on medium speed for 2 to 3 minutes. Add the sifted ingredients and mix until thoroughly combined. Pour the batter into 2 lightly greased 8-by-4-inch loaf pans.

Place the pans on a baking sheet and bake for 60 to 70 minutes, or until the cake springs back when lightly pressed. Let cool in the pans for 10 to 15 minutes. Turn the cakes out onto wire racks to finish cooling.

Slice the cakes with a serrated bread knife. Enjoy as is, or serve with whipped cream flavored with sugar and cinnamon.

Chef's Tip: To measure honey easily, oil the inside of the measuring cup. Then the honey will not stick.

BASIC INGREDIENTS, TECHNIQUES, AND RECIPES

BASIC INGREDIENTS

MEXICAN INGREDIENTS

There is a wider variety of Mexican ingredients and dried chilies available now than ever before. This short glossary will help you select and find ingredients to use in your favorite Mexican dishes. Most of them are available at Latino markets or specialty foods stores.

CHILIES

When working with chilies, wear rubber gloves, don't touch your eyes or other sensitive areas, and wash your tools, work surface, and hands carefully and thoroughly with hot soapy water. (This caution applies to all chilies.)

Habaneros may be purchased either fresh or dried. They are one of the hottest of all chilies. Habaneros occupy a special place in the cooking of the Yucatán. Believed to be originally from Havana, they are now cultivated extensively in Yucatán and are a signature flavor of that cuisine.

Chipotle chilies are dried smoked jalapeño chilies.

Ancho chilies are dried poblano chilies, with a prune-raisin flavor.

Pasilla chilies are dried black chilaca chilies, with a tannin-licorice-tobacco flavor.

Guajillo chilies are dried red chilies with a tannin-cherry flavor.

OTHER MEXICAN INGREDIENTS

Masa harina is a flour made from sun-dried corn.

Banana leaves are often sold in 1-pound packages. They freeze well, so stock up when you find them. Do not eat banana leaves.

Mexican oregano is less sweet than Mediterranean or Greek oregano. If Mexican oregano isn't available, the best alternative is fresh oregano. Use about double the amount of the dried oregano called for in the recipe.

Epazote is a wild herb used as a flavoring, especially for black beans. It is available fresh or dried. In its raw state, some say it has an aroma similar to kerosene, but after cooking the flavor becomes quite pleasant. Some people describe the taste as being similar to the smell of the desert after rain. There is no real substitute for epazote.

VANILLA BEANS

To extract the flavorful seeds, carefully split the vanilla bean pod lengthwise with the tip of a paring knife. Use a teaspoon to scrape the tiny black sticky seeds from the interior. One teaspoon good-quality vanilla extract may be substituted for the seeds scraped from 1 vanilla bean.

BASIC TECHNIQUES

BEAN COOKERY

Rinse and sort the dried beans to remove any stones or discolored beans. Then, use one of the following methods to prepare the beans for cooking.

LONG-SOAK METHOD

Soak dried beans overnight in cold water to cover by 2 inches. Drain and rinse before using as directed in the recipe.

SHORT-SOAK METHOD

Place dried beans in a pot and add water to cover by 2 inches. Bring to a boil, then remove from heat and let soak for 1 hour. Drain and rinse the beans before continuing.

TO COOK BEANS

Put the soaked beans in a large pot and add water to cover by 2 inches. Bring to a boil over high heat. Reduce heat to medium and simmer the beans, uncovered, until they are tender, about 2 hours. Cooking times will vary depending on the beans. Add onions, carrots, celery, bay leaves, or other herbs as the beans cook, if desired. Add salt during the last half hour of cooking, if desired.

Canned beans may be used in place of home-cooked beans. Drain and rinse them before use. If the cooking liquid from the beans is called for in the recipe, substitute broth or water. Canned beans are already tender, so be careful not to overcook.

BLANCHING AND PARBOILING VEGETABLES

Bring a large pot of water to a boil. Add the vegetables and cook for 3 to 8 minutes. The cooking time will vary depending on the size and texture of the vegetables. Drop the vegetables into ice water to stop the cooking (known as "shocking"). Drain and keep chilled until ready to use.

GREEN VEGETABLES

Green vegetables (asparagus, asparagus tips, fiddlehead ferns, broccoli, peas, zucchini, etc.) are properly blanched when they take on a vibrant bright green color.

ROOT VEGETABLES AND PEARL ONIONS

Root vegetables (potatoes, carrots, parsnips, and so on) and pearl onions are generally blanched until they are cooked two thirds of the way though, or parboiled. To check for doneness, cut through root vegetables or onions. The outer two thirds should be tender, but the inner core still uncooked.

Pearl onions are easier to peel after they have been blanched and "shocked."

LEEKS

To clean leeks: Cut away the root ends and the light green and dark green portions of the leaves. Cut the leeks in half lengthwise and rinse thoroughly under cool running water until all traces of dirt and sand are removed.

PEELED, SEEDED, AND CHOPPED TOMATOES

Professional chefs refer to peeled, seeded, and chopped tomatoes as tomato concassé. To prepare them, bring a pot of water to a rolling boil. Fill a bowl with ice water and have it near the stove. Core the tomatoes and score an "x" through the skin on the bottom of each. Submerge a few tomatoes at a time in the boiling water for 15 to 30 seconds. Using a slotted spoon, transfer the tomatoes to the ice water. Drain the tomatoes and pull the skin away. Cut slicing tomatoes in half crosswise. Plum (Roma) tomatoes should be halved from top to bottom. Squeeze or scrape out the seeds and chop the flesh.

ROASTED GARLIC

Wrap a whole garlic bulb in aluminum foil and place in a preheated 350°F oven. Roast for 45 minutes to 1 hour.

If the whole head is called for, cut off the top and squeeze out the garlic. Or, pull off as many cloves as you need and squeeze out the flesh.

Cover and store any unused roasted garlic in the refrigerator for up to 1 week.

ROASTED PEPPERS

Roasted peppers are available in most food markets in cans or jars. If you want to roast your own, begin by brushing the whole peppers with olive oil. Place the peppers on top of a grill preheated to high heat, or under a preheated broiler, or directly in the flame of a gas burner, turning occasionally until charred all over. Alternatively, place the peppers on a baking sheet in a preheated 350°F oven and roast for about 30 to 45 minutes, or until the skin puckers and the peppers are quite soft. Place the peppers in a paper or plastic bag, close the bag, and let steam for 5 minutes. Remove from the bag and peel by hand. Remove the stem and seeds and cut as desired.

CLARIFIED BUTTER

Cut unsalted butter into pieces and put them in a heavy saucepan. Melt over medium to low heat until the butter separates into layers; do not stir. Skim the foam off the butter and carefully ladle the clear butter into a clean container, leaving the solids and milky liquid at the bottom of the pan. Chefs often use a blend of half oil and half clarified butter when they sauté or panfry foods.

SHAVED PARMESAN

Use a vegetable peeler to shave thin pieces from a block of Parmesan. Shave the "curls" only in one direction for best results. If a full block of Parmesan is not available, grated Parmesan is a good alternative. The flavor will be the same, although the appearance and texture will be different.

CROUTONS

To make 1 cup of plain croutons: Remove the crusts from 4 slices of bread. Cut the bread into cubes and place on a baking sheet. Bake in a preheated 275°F oven, stirring occasionally, until light golden brown.

To make 1 cup of seasoned croutons: Sauté 1 cup of dried bread cubes in 2 tablespoons of vegetable oil with 1 teaspoon minced garlic until golden brown.

TOASTED BREAD CRUMBS

Preheat the oven to 375°F. Remove the crusts from a 1-pound loaf of peasant bread and cut into 1-inch cubes. Place the bread cubes in a food processor and pulse until coarsely ground. Measure the crumbs by the cupful and pour them into a bowl. For each 2 cups of crumbs, add 1 tablespoon of olive oil, ¼ teaspoon of salt, and a pinch of freshly ground pepper. Toss to coat the crumbs well, then spread them on a baking sheet and bake, tossing occasionally, for about 5 minutes, or until crumbs are dry and light golden brown. Toasted bread crumbs may be stored in a freezer bag in the freezer and used as garnish for pasta or as a crumb topping for stuffed vegetables.

TOASTED NUTS

Toast nuts by placing them in a cast-iron skillet or on baking sheet in a 350°F oven. Toast for 5 to 8 minutes, stirring occasionally to ensure even coloring. The cooking time will vary according to the size of the nuts being toasted.

TRUSSING A CHICKEN

To truss a chicken, use stout cotton twine, referred to as butcher's twine, to tie the chicken into a compact shape. Run the twine around the ends of the legs, and over the thighs, in the fold between the thighs and the breast. Catch the wings with the twine, and then tie securely. Your butcher can do this for you, if you prefer.

CITRUS ZEST

Citrus zest (the peel of lemons, limes, oranges, and grape-fruits) that has been julienned for garnish should be blanched before serving to remove any bitterness. Place the julienned zest in a medium saucepan and cover with cold water. Bring to a boil and then drain off the water. Repeat this process 3 more times. Drain thoroughly and set aside.

PASSION FRUIT JUICE

Passion fruit juice is available at specialty or natural foods stores. To make it yourself, cut open 3 to 4 passion fruits for every ¼ cup of juice (the more wrinkled the better) and scoop out the pulp. Press it through a fine-meshed sieve to extract the juice and remove the seeds.

TEMPERING CHOCOLATE

The process of heating chocolate to 115°F and then cool-ing it to 90°F is known as "tempering." Tempering gives chocolate a lasting gloss and helps it set so it snaps crisply. As you dip food into chocolate, the temperature should remain within a degree or two of 90°F. The chocolate can be gently rewarmed to 90°F, but if you warm the chocolate above 90°F, you must go through the entire tempering process again.

RECIPES

BROWN RICE
Makes about 1 cup

⅔ cup water
⅓ cup brown long-grain rice
Pinch of salt

Combine all the ingredients in a small saucepan and bring to a boil over high heat. Reduce heat to low, cover, and simmer for about 40 minutes, or until the water is absorbed and the rice is tender. Remove the rice from the heat and let stand for 5 minutes. Fluff gently with a fork.

HERBED OIL
Makes 2 cups

Use the oil for the recipe on page 41. Or, serve it as a dip or spread for peasant-style bread, drizzle it on vegetable soup, or use it to replace plain oil in your favorite vinaigrette recipe.

½ bunch parsley
2 cups olive oil

Combine the parsley and oil in a blender or food processor and purée for about 15 seconds. Strain through cheesecloth and store in a tightly covered jar in the refrigerator for up to 1 week. Let the oil come to room temperature before using.

BROWN VEAL STOCK
Makes about 1 cup

4 pounds meaty veal bones
1 large onion, coarsely chopped
1 carrot, coarsely chopped
1 celery stalk, coarsely chopped
2 tablespoons tomato paste
12 cups water
5 to 6 peppercorns
3 to 4 parsley stems
1 thyme sprig

Preheat the oven to 400°F. Place the bones in a roasting pan and roast, turning occasionally, for about 20 minutes, or until evenly browned. Transfer the bones to a large stockpot.

Pour off the fat from the roasting pan. Place the pan on the stovetop over medium heat and add the onion, carrots, and celery. Cook, stirring occasionally, for 5 minutes. Add the tomato paste and cook, stirring constantly, until it begins to brown and has a sweet aroma. Add the vegetables and tomato paste to the bones in the stockpot. Add 1 cup of the water to the roasting pan and return to heat. Stir until most of the pan drippings have been loosened. Pour into the stockpot.

Add the remaining 11 cups water, peppercorns, parsley, and thyme to the stockpot and simmer, uncovered, for 4 to 5 hours, skimming every 15 minutes to remove the foam that rises to the surface. Ladle the broth through a sieve into a clean container.

To store the broth, cool it quickly by placing the container in a sink filled with ice water. Stir the broth as it cools, then transfer it to storage containers. As the broth cools, the fat will rise to the surface and act as a protective seal. Store in the refrigerator for up to 5 days, or in the freezer up to 3 months. Label and date the containers clearly before putting them in the freezer. Remove the fat layer before using the broth.

CHICKEN BROTH
Makes 8 cups

The coagulated chicken fat on the top of chilled broth is perfect for use in the Passover and Rosh Hashanah recipes in this book. Chicken fat is also called *schmaltz*.

4 pounds chicken bones and parts (about 2 birds)
10 cups cold water, plus more as needed
1 large onion, thinly sliced
1 carrot, thinly sliced
1 stalk celery, thinly sliced
5 to 6 peppercorns
3 to 4 parsley stems
1 bay leaf
1 thyme sprig

Put the chicken bones and parts in a large stockpot. Add water to cover the chicken by 2 inches. Bring the water slowly to a boil over medium heat. Skim off any foam that rises to the surface. Reduce heat to low and simmer, uncovered, for about 1½ to 2 hours. Add the remaining ingredients and simmer, skimming the surface as necessary, for 1 hour.

Ladle the broth through a sieve into a clean container. To store the broth, cool it quickly by placing the container in a sink filled with ice water. Stir the broth as it cools, then transfer it to smaller storage containers if desired. As the broth cools, the fat will rise to the surface and act as a protective seal. Store in the refrigerator up to 5 days, or in the freezer up to 3 months. Label and date the containers clearly before putting them in the freezer. Remove the fat layer before using the broth.

FISH BROTH
Makes 8 cups

3 pounds bones from lean white fish
8 cups cold water
3 celery stalks, finely chopped
1 small onion, finely chopped
2 parsnips, finely chopped
5 peppercorns
3 parsley stems
1 bay leaf
1 thyme sprig

Combine all the ingredients in a large stockpot over high heat. Bring to a boil, then reduce heat to a simmer. Cook, uncovered, for 30 minutes, skimming every 5 minutes to remove the foam that rises to the surface. Ladle the broth through a sieve into a clean container.

To store the broth, cool it quickly by placing the container in a sink filled with ice water. Stir the broth as it cools, then transfer it to smaller storage containers if desired. Store in the refrigerator up to 5 days, or in the freezer for up to 3 months. Label and date the containers clearly before putting them into the freezer.

DUCK BROTH
Makes 1 gallon

This recipe will produce a good quantity of rich, flavorful broth. Keep the broth not required for the sauce on page 10 to make into soup.

Reserved legs and carcasses from 4 ducks
½ cup dry red wine
1 gallon cold water, plus more if needed
2 tablespoons vegetable oil
4 onions, coarsely chopped
2 large carrots, coarsely chopped
3 celery stalks, coarsely chopped
2 parsnips, coarsely chopped
10 peppercorns
2 bay leaves
2 thyme sprigs
3 parsley stems

Preheat the oven to 375°F. Separate the thighs and drumsticks. Use a cleaver or poultry shears to cut the carcass into 3-inch pieces. Place the duck pieces in a roasting pan large enough to hold them in a single layer. Roast for 20 to 30 minutes, turning occasionally, until evenly browned. Transfer the duck pieces to a large stockpot.

Pour off the fat from the roasting pan. Add the wine and stir with a wooden spoon to release all the pan drippings. Add this liquid to the stockpot with the duck. Add the water to cover the bones by 3 inches. Bring to a boil over high heat, then reduce heat to a low to establish a gentle simmer. Simmer, uncovered, for 2½ hours, skimming every 15 minutes to remove the foam that rises to the surface.

Meanwhile, heat the oil in large sauté pan over medium heat. Add the onions, carrots, celery, and parsnips and sauté until the vegetables are browned, about 15 to 20 minutes. Add the vegetables, peppercorns, bay leaves, thyme, and parsley stems to the broth and simmer 1 hour longer. Ladle the broth through a sieve into a clean container. To store the broth, cool it quickly by placing the container in a sink filled with ice water. Stir the broth as it cools, then transfer it to smaller storage containers if desired. As the broth cools, the fat will rise to the surface and act as a protective seal. Store in the refrigerator for up to 5 days, or in the freezer up to 3 months. Label and date the containers clearly before putting them in the freezer. Remove the fat layer before using the broth.

VEGETABLE BROTH
Makes 8 cups

The vegetables listed in the ingredients below should be thought of as suggestions. Feel free to add other vegetables, as long as they will not give the finished stock a strong odor or color (such as beets, cooking greens and cabbage).

2 teaspoons olive oil
1 to 2 garlic cloves, minced
2 teaspoons minced shallot
8 cups water
½ cup dry white wine or vermouth (optional)
1 large onion, thinly sliced
1 leek, thinly sliced
1 celery stalk, thinly sliced on the diagonal
1 carrot, thinly sliced
1 parsnip, thinly sliced
1 cup thinly sliced broccoli stems
1 cup sliced fennel with some tops
4 to 5 peppercorns
½ teaspoon juniper berries
1 bay leaf
1 thyme spring, or ¼ teaspoon dried thyme, crumbled

Heat the oil in a large stockpot over medium heat. Add the garlic and shallot, and sauté, stirring frequently, until they are translucent, 3 to 4 minutes. Add the remaining ingredients and bring the broth to a boil. Reduce heat to a simmer and cook for about 30 to 40 minutes, or until the broth has a good, rich flavor. Ladle the broth through a sieve into a clean container.

To store the broth, cool it quickly by placing the container in a sink filled with ice water. Stir the broth as it cools, then transfer it to smaller storage containers if desired. Store in the refrigerator up to 5 days, or in the freezer up to 3 months. Label and date the containers clearly before putting them into the freezer.

TART SHELL
Makes one 12-inch tart shell

½ cup (1 stick) chilled unsalted butter, diced
⅓ cup powdered sugar
1 egg
Finely grated zest of ½ lemon
Pinch of salt
2 cups sifted cake flour, plus more for dusting

Preheat the oven to 350°F. Combine the butter, sugar, egg, lemon zest, and salt in a food processor. Process for about 10 seconds, or until small crumbs form. Add the flour and pulse until the dough becomes lumpy but has not yet formed a ball. To mix the dough by hand, cream together the butter and sugar in a large bowl. Mix in the eggs and vanilla until very well blended. Add the flour and mix until just combined.

Remove the dough to a lightly floured work surface and knead gently by hand until the dough just comes together. Place the dough between 2 pieces of waxed or parchment paper and roll it to a ¼-inch thickness and 14-inch diameter. Chill in the refrigerator for 5 minutes. The dough may be prepared, wrapped in plastic, and refrigerated up to 3 days in advance. Let the dough sit at room temperature for 15 to 20 minutes to soften slightly before rolling it.

Meanwhile, butter a 12-inch tart pan or spray it with cooking spray. Remove the top layer of paper from the dough and flip the dough over into the prepared pan.

Carefully fit the dough into the pan and cut off the excess by rolling the rolling pin over the edges of the pan. Prick the entire surface of the dough with the tines of a fork. Cut a 14-inch-diameter circle from parchment paper and make 1-inch-deep snips at ½-inch intervals around the edges. Line the dough with the paper circle and fill it with the dried beans or pie weights.

Bake the dough for 12 minutes. Remove paper and beans or weights and bake another 5 to 7 minutes, if necessary, to brown the bottom crust.

CHOCOLATE SPONGE CAKE
Makes three 10-inch round layers

Since only 1 cake layer is required for the tart, wrap the remaining 2 layers well in plastic wrap and freeze for up to 2 weeks.

8 egg yolks
½ cup sugar
Pinch of salt
Finely grated zest of ½ lemon
2 teaspoons vanilla extract
⅓ cup unsweetened cocoa powder
1 cup all-purpose or cake flour
¼ cup cornstarch
4 egg whites

Preheat the oven to 350°F. Trace three 10-inch circles on sheets of parchment paper and line baking sheets with the paper.

Combine the egg yolks, 2 tablespoons of the sugar, the salt, lemon zest, vanilla extract, and cocoa powder in a large bowl. Whisk until blended. Sift the flour and cornstarch together onto a piece of parchment or waxed paper.

Combine the whites and the remaining 6 tablespoons of the sugar in a large bowl. Using an electric mixer or a whisk, beat the whites until stiff but glossy peaks form.

Gently fold the egg yolk mixture into the whipped whites, then fold in the sifted flour mixture. Transfer the mixture to a piping bag fitted with a ⅜-inch-wide tip. Pipe the mixture in a spiral onto the parchment paper, completely filling each traced circle.

Bake for 3 to 4 minutes. Transfer the cakes, still on the paper, to a cool surface or a counter. Remove them from the parchment once they have cooled completely.

INDEX

Cuisinart

Cuisinart is proud to sponsor Public Broadcasting's

"Cooking Secrets of The CIA".

When Cuisinart introduced home cooks to the world-famous food processor,

we shared a secret professional cooks had known for years.

Today, we continue to strive for culinary excellence,

and this is why we are pleased to be part of

"Cooking Secrets of The CIA".

The Culinary Institute of America dedicates itself to

provide the finest culinary education in the world.

Cuisinart® Professional Series Food Processors

The Cuisinart® Pro Food Prep Center does it all — from stir-fries and pasta dishes to cakes and cookies. It simplifies your life and makes cooking a pleasure. Efficient enough for small amounts but large enough for entertaining, the Pro Food Prep Center comes with everything you need to make great meals. It features Cuisinart's exclusive large feed tube and compact baking covers, precision slicing and shredding discs, a whisk attachment and how-to video. Clean-up is easy with dishwasher-safe parts.

Coffee Bar™ Flavor System Coffeemakers

bring coffee bar brewing technology to your home. The 12-cup Automatic Coffeemaker features a self-cleaning mode, adjustable shut off and holding temperature. A full line of coffeemakers is available in white or black models.

Coffee Bar™ Coffee Grinder

complements coffee enjoyment. Stainless steel blades and bowl provide superior grinding. Measuring coffee is easy in the grinder's cover with 2- and 4-cup markings.

SmartPower™ Hand Mixers

offer a powerful 220-watt motor and super-sized beaters that cut through cold sticks of butter. The 7-speed Electronic LED model has 3 low mix speeds for controlled folding and mixing of dry ingredients. A professional Chef's Whisk speeds whipping tasks.

Cuisinart® Blenders

are powerful and convenient to use. These full-function blenders crush ice instantly, mix salsas, purée soups and much more. The hinged fill cap doubles as a 1- or 2-ounce measure to add ingredients without stopping the blending action. The Vari-Speed Pro™ blender comes with a lighted variable speed control and extra stainless jar for added convenience.

Heat Surround™ Motor Rise™ Electronic Toaster

has a 2-inch wide slot to toast everything evenly. Heating walls actually move to surround the thinnest or thickest slice — even holds whole bagels. The Motor Rise™ feature gently raises and lowers even delicate muffins. TruThaw™ Variable Defrost uses less heat so bread doesn't dry out.

Cuisinart® counter top appliances and cookware are designed to be useful, versatile and easy-to-use. Crafted from the highest quality materials, each product offers the best value for today's cook.

Endless time-consuming tasks become effortless; delicious meals become possible with Cuisinart products at your side.

Our food preparation appliances come complete with recipe collections that guide you every step of the way.

You can trust Cuisinart to make your time in the kitchen more rewarding...and fun!

Cuisinart

Cuisinart® Everyday Collection™ Cookware and Stick Free Stainless Non-Stick Cookware

Cuisinart® Everyday Collection™ Cookware

Originally inspired by great chefs, Cuisinart® Everyday Collection™ Cookware is as rugged as it is beautiful. Its 18/10 mirror-finish stainless steel with copper bottom construction cooks better and faster. Stay-cool handles, a stick-resistant cooking surface and easy dishwasher clean-up make Cuisinart® cookware a pleasure to own and to use.

18/10 Stainless Steel with Copper

Cuisinart® Stick Free Stainless Non-Stick Cookware

Cuisinart has combined non-stick convenience with professional quality cookware setting a new standard in non-stick cookware.

It contains no aluminum and is designed for flavorful, healthful cooking. Through a special Excalibur® Multi-Layer System, stainless steel is actually built into the non-stick material for superior durability.

Available in a variety of useful shapes and sizes, Cuisinart® Stick Free Stainless offers Cuisinart quality with non-stick convenience.

Excalibur® Multi-Layer System
18/10 Stainless Steel
Pure Copper
18/10 Stainless Steel